GEOFFREY TREASE

LONDON

A CONCISE HISTORY

with 205 illustrations

CHARLES SCRIBNER'S SONS

NEW YORK

For
Philippa MacLiesh
George Astley
Victor Bonham-Carter
three good friends who have so often
brightened my visits to the city

Contents

The Roman City

There is 'no valid reason for supposing that London existed prior to AD 43.' Such was the conclusion of Sir Mortimer Wheeler in the Royal Commission Report of 1928, and up to the time of writing, despite the very considerable archaeological discoveries of almost half a century, no evidence has turned up to alter that view. The idea of a pre-Roman city is best left to imaginative medieval authors like the Benedictine monk, Geoffrey of Monmouth, who perpetuated the legend of a town built by a Trojan refugee, Brutus, and called 'New Troy', to be subsequently renamed 'London' after an equally shadowy character, King Lud.

When the Romans conquered Britain they noticed no such place, and, since they had to force the crossing of the Thames in that very neighbourhood, a town on the north bank could hardly have escaped mention in the records. The truth seems to be that an ancient British London would have been both impracticable and pointless. The foundation of a city on that site depended on geographical factors which the Britons lacked the engineering skill to exploit: they could not have bridged so wide a tidal river. Nor, if it had been technically possible, would it have been worth the trouble: though the Britons certainly traded with continental Europe, there was not the volume of traffic which, in Roman times and every period since then, made London a natural port. It is easy now to explain London's situation as inevitably pinpointed by these two considerations – the lowest point where the Thames could be bridged, the highest that could be reached by vessels using the flow of the tide – but such considerations did not mean much before the coming of the Romans, able to build not only that bridge but a network of roads fanning out from it in all directions, and drawing a hitherto independent and little-known island into the whole unified economic community of the Empire.

One geological change in the subsequent nineteen centuries has to be mentioned. South-eastern England has tilted downwards and the water level has risen. Today, the tide runs more than twenty miles further up-river, to Teddington. When the site of London was chosen, the highest tidal point was in the neighbourhood of our present London Bridge. In any case, unconfined by its modern embankments and less suddenly swollen by modern town and country drainage, the Thames was altogether wider, shallower and more sluggish, with practicable fords that were quite adequate for British needs. This alteration in conditions makes it even easier to understand why Roman London came to be established at this particular spot.

It makes it easier also to visualize the scene described by Dio Cassius in his history of Rome, when he tells how the Britons fell back before the advancing

Opposite Memorial to M. Favonius Facilis, centurion of the XXth Legion, probably killed in Boudicca's rebellion. He holds the vine staff marking his rank.

troops of Aulus Plautius in the summer of 43. Using fords known to them, the natives retreated north of the Thames 'near where it enters the ocean and at high water forms a lake', a description which very neatly fits what we now call the Pool of London. When the Romans tried to follow, they not unnaturally got into difficulties and some of them had to swim for it. To explain how they eventually won a foothold on the north bank, Dio Cassius airily says that some 'got over by a bridge a short distance upstream', and thereby the learned Roman senator created the legend of a pre-Roman bridge, for which there is no other evidence and against which there is every argument of improbability.

One must not be disrespectful to ancient historians. Though they had neither the mountains of source-material nor the academic discipline of their modern equivalents, they were not without records or regard for accuracy. All the same, Dio Cassius was writing a century and a half after the event, and it is far easier to see how he came to fall into this error than to accept his all-too-convenient bridge as genuine. The most likely explanation is that he merely anticipated its existence by a few weeks. When he wrote his history, either in Rome or even further away from Britain, there had been a bridge at London ever since anyone could remember, and most likely since that very year of the invasion. There is an excellent reason for supposing that the Romans built one immediately. Aulus Plautius, we know, deliberately delayed his advance north of the Thames, so that his master, the Emperor Claudius, could come over from the Continent and enjoy the personal triumph of entering the main British town, Camulodunum, or Colchester. During the weeks of waiting, what would be more natural than the construction of a bridge, which, as we know from Julius Caesar's earlier achievements on the Rhine, the Roman engineers could accomplish in a matter of days? Claudius would not have been best pleased if invited to cross the Thames by ford or boat, especially since his retinue included elephants.

Nature had obligingly provided two beds of firm gravel, one on either bank, ideally placed to take the ends of the bridge, whereas downstream stretched only the treacherous tidal mud. All we can say for certain is that, if the Romans did not build a temporary or permanent bridge immediately, they must have done so soon afterwards, and once it existed its convenience was so obvious that a town mushroomed into existence. The north bank was more suitable than the south. There was the high ground, on which St Paul's and the City stand to this day. And there was the Walbrook, now only a name, one of London's vanished tributary rivers, but at that date a clear stream taking craft of a certain size, its banks destined to become the most pleasant and fashionable residential area of the new Londinium.

That city grew spontaneously, not from any political or military decision. Claudius made Colchester the capital of his newly conquered province, and the main garrisons were located, as the legions pushed north and west, at Lincoln, York and Gloucester. But London inevitably was the nodal point of the long straight roads that led to them, and it was on London wharves, just below the bridge, that the flat-bottomed trading ships were soon loading and unloading their cargoes. In the short space of eighteen years, when Queen Boudicca came raging out of East Anglia in foredoomed rebellion, London had become, in the words of Tacitus, 'a great trading centre, full of merchants'.

Roman helmet, found at Colchester but similar to those of the Cripplegate garrison.

Those merchants must have been largely British – collaborators, Boudicca and her ferocious Iceni tribesmen considered them – with a number of Gauls and other enterprising newcomers. Few residents of Roman London are likely to have come from Rome, or even Italy.

Nor could there have been any legionaries, for London had no military status, and at that time the commander-in-chief, Suetonius Paulinus, was far away campaigning in Wales. He rode back with his cavalry, hell for leather, to save London from the disaster that had already overwhelmed Colchester. He relied on infantry marching from Gloucester to meet him. They did not come and he had to abandon London to the first of the many catastrophes that were to befall it in the course of its long history. The defenceless town was looted and burnt. The inhabitants, who seem not to have fled for the most part, but to have trusted naïvely in the good will of the rebels, who were fellow Celts albeit of a different tribe, were slaughtered with atrocities worthy of the twentieth century. The extent of the London massacre can only be guessed. The total death-roll for Colchester, London and St Albans was reckoned at seventy thousand. Many skulls have been discovered along the old course of the Walbrook during building operations near the Mansion House, and these may well date from Boudicca's visit, for decapitation was a favourite practice with the Celtic warriors. Of the fire there is even more certain evidence in a stratum of reddish fire-hardened debris, containing pottery and coins of the period.

From these ashes a new and better city rose. Julius Classicianus was appointed procurator or civil governor of the province, apparently a humane and statesmanlike administrator who did much to check the military reprisals and conciliate the population. He seems to have preferred London to Colchester as his headquarters. The shattered fragments of his tomb, dug up at different times and at last triumphantly fitted together, show that he was buried

Sixty years after the Roman invasion, Londinium probably looked like this: a trading centre and the focal point for the long, straight military roads.

9

The Romans built to last.
Part of the two-mile city wall
survives in St Alphage
churchyard, in the City.

The Emperor Hadrian
inspected Britain in AD 122:
a portrait head recovered from
the Thames.

there. Several other finds, such as a wooden writing-tablet now in the British Museum, inscribed PROC AUG DEDERUNT BRIT PROV, signifying 'issued by the Imperial Procurators of the Province of Britain', suggest, if they do not prove, that London quickly became the financial centre of the province. It seems likely that other departments were increasingly transferred there and that, by the early part of the second century, London had become the effective capital.

As such, it could not be left defenceless. A stone fort was built at Cripplegate on the north-western edge of the city. It covered twelve acres, much less than the main legionary depots elsewhere but enough to accommodate fifteen hundred to two thousand troops. This fort was later incorporated into the wall, built towards the close of the second century, which – we now know – eventually ran along the river as well as the other three sides of the city, enclosing an area of 325 acres and making London one of the half-dozen largest provincial centres in the Western Empire.

Its development must have been at its height when Hadrian visited Britain in 122 on one of his indefatigable imperial tours of inspection. An avid sight-seer and especially a connoisseur of architecture, the Emperor would surely have admired the great basilica, erected about forty years earlier, near where Leadenhall Market was to stand in after times. Over five hundred feet long, a complex of town hall, community centre, law courts and exchange, this remarkable building was surpassed only by the Basilica Ulpia in Rome itself. That London should require anything on this scale, only a few feet shorter than the present St Paul's Cathedral, underlines the importance of the young city.

A few years later, about AD 125, came the second of London's many great fires, this time accidental, and devastating a fifth of the area. Probably it acted only as a stimulus to development. Hadrian's peaceful reign was a great period for town planning and it was his policy to raise provincial standards to those of Rome.

The wall was not added until about the year 200, when the long era of Roman peace and order had closed with the death of Marcus Aurelius and the shadow of barbarism was beginning to creep across the Empire. London's wall was two miles long, perhaps twenty feet high, and seven or eight feet thick. It was built mainly of ragstone, quarried in Kent and brought up by barge from the Medway, altogether about a million cubic feet of stone.

One of those barges was discovered in modern times, preserved in the Black-friars mud and still containing its ragstone cargo. The dating provides a good example of the detective methods followed by the archaeologist and anticipates the layman's instinctive question, 'How can they tell?' In the mast-step of the vessel lay a copper coin, obviously placed there for luck at the time of building, in accordance with a superstition still sometimes observed by yacht-builders today. The 'tail' side showed the goddess of Fortune, appropriately holding a ship's rudder. The coin was one of Domitian's, datable at AD 88 or 89, but well worn by the time it was put into the new-built barge. The presence of second-century pottery roughly indicated the period during which the vessel was in service before some mishap sent it to the bottom of the river. These clues are consistent with many others, coins and pottery, discovered in the wall itself.

Wooden barge dating from Roman times. Preserved in the mud off Blackfriars, it still contained its cargo of Kentish ragstone for the city wall.

Clearly it was under construction for some considerable time, and AD 200 is a very fair approximation.

Within the girdle of this wall stood a city of perhaps forty-five thousand inhabitants. It was a multi-racial community, comprising native Britons, their Gallic cousins from over the Channel, and a not inconsiderable sprinkling of people from Italy, Spain, North Africa and the eastern provinces of the Empire. Latin was the official language and the medium of the upper classes. It was probably understood at all levels in London, though not in remoter parts of Britain, much as English would later serve in Calcutta but not in every Indian village. We know from Tacitus that the toga was worn widely as formal dress. It was far from ideal for the British climate, but the true Roman could be very contemptuous of such barbaric garments as breeches, and it is interesting to know that the earliest London businessman, like his counterpart in more recent days, sacrificed comfort to conformity.

There was comfort, however, in the best houses, built on piles or reinforced foundations along the Walbrook, stone houses with mosaics and marble from Mediterranean quarries, and warmed with under-floor hypocausts against the Thames Valley chills. Other Londoners lived more simply. They had thatched, timber-frame houses, with plastered walls in crude colours, mustard-yellow or ox-blood. The floor would be of tiles, concrete or merely earth, and the only form of heating was a brazier. This was, as elsewhere in the Empire, a slave-based society. The slave trade, indeed, was a profitable part of London's business. So everyday life varied greatly with the individual, from the high-ranking civil servant and the merchant, drinking imported wine from exquisite drinking-cups, down to the humble craftsman and the manual labourer.

Bronze statuette of a British slave. Like other Roman cities, London had its flourishing slave trade.

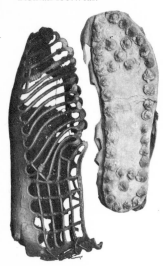

Rarely, even leather has survived. Examples of Roman footwear.

Those lives can be pictured, or glimpsed at least, from the countless relics, usually small, often homely, almost always informative, that survive in the showcases of our museums. There we can see the knives and spoons with which they ate, the brooches and studs, the hairpins and toilet sets with which the women beautified themselves, the clerk's ink-pot, stylus and writing-tablet, the shopkeeper's balance, the docker's crowbar, the waterman's boat-hook, the smith's pincers. Even leather has survived. We can still gaze at a shoe or a sandal or, most evocative of all, the so-called 'bikini', that skimpy loin-covering in which some girl displayed herself almost nineteen centuries ago.

It is all tantalizingly anonymous – and the few names accidentally pre-served for us only tease us the more since we know nothing beyond them. A tile dug up in Newgate Street is scratched with the inscription, 'For the past thirteen days Austalis has gone off on his own.' A sheet of lead, found near Moorgate Street and once nailed up, inscription facing the wall, with seven mystical nails, carries the beginning of a virulent invocation: 'I curse Tretia Maria, her life and mind and memory, her liver and lungs combined, and her words, thoughts and memory. So may she be powerless to tell those things that are hid. . . .' One longs to know more of Austalis and Tretia Maria, what they had been doing and what happened to them. At least these pro-voking fragments bring the warmth of human feeling into the cold bits and pieces set out under the museum glass.

There was, alas, no archetypal Pepys, jotting down in cursive Latin a day-by-day chronicle of Londinium's scandals and intrigues. Britain never pro-duced a school of late classical authors to match those of Gaul and North Africa, so that the written evidence for those four centuries amounts to little more than inscriptions on coins and monuments and a few graffiti. Roman London had no Samuel Johnson. Even if it had a Dick Whittington, we have no record of him. How these people lived, and what their mental processes were, can be deduced only from what we know of Roman provincial society in general.

It was on the whole stable to the point of stagnation, with no encouragement for originality, speculation or more than ordinary commercial enterprise. The authoritarian central government and its efficient bureaucracy left little scope for political activity even at local level. Reluctant townsmen often had to be detailed for municipal offices that nobody wanted to hold. Slave labour removed the incentive to seek technical improvements, let alone scientific discovery. Orthodox religion – emperor-worship and lip service to the old Olympian gods and goddesses – was unemotional and devoid of spiritual satisfaction. People who craved that were drawn to the mystical cults from the East. Isis and Cybele had their London devotees, and so, clearly, had Chris-tianity, for there was a Bishop of London, Restitutus, at the Council of Arles in 314, only a year after Constantine's official recognition of the Church. But the surviving architectural evidence cannot compare with the remarkable Temple of Mithras, a rival cult with certain moral and mystical affinities.

The immense public interest in this discovery in 1954 has obscured, for those who did not visit the site, the fact that the Mithraeum was a relatively small building, designed for only a few dozen worshippers. It was not unlike

'Countless relics . . . often homely, almost always informative.' Roman imported pottery, knives and skewers found in London.

These wooden writing tablets were probably 'Government issue', and suggest that London soon became the province's financial centre: the stamp states 'issued by the Imperial Procurators of the Province of Britain'.

a college chapel, narrow, with a raised sanctuary in an apse at one end, and swing doors at the other, the congregation apparently facing each other, as in choir-stalls, from colonnaded aisles. Mithraism was for the few. To suppose that all Roman Londoners worshipped this Persian deity would be as mistaken as for future archaeologists, excavating the Athenaeum, to conclude that every twentieth-century Londoner was a member. Mithraism attracted the army officer and the well-to-do merchant. Women were barred. There

A late third-century relief from the Mithraeum shows a figure wearing a Phrygian cap. Mithraism was an eastern religion favoured by a middle-class minority.

was an emphasis on honour and on fidelity in bargains. The modern City derives some understandable satisfaction from the evidence that it was one of the first religions practised on the site.

Such, then, was London in the first four centuries of our era: a high-walled city north of the Thames, with busy wharves and bridge, a fortified barracks at one corner, a huge basilica and forum, temples, baths, shops and houses, in streets laid out to a typically ordered Roman plan.

Few sensational historic events disturbed what might have seemed, to our sensibilities, the monotony of those years in a big but rather remote provincial centre. The self-sufficient Londoners can scarcely have realized that the decline of the Roman Empire was well under way. Business was either good or bad. Only occasionally, when civil strife arose in the mainland provinces, disrupting communications, did great affairs ruffle this quiet backwater.

A particularly disturbed period came in 287. The Emperor in the West, Maximian, fell out with the admiral of the Channel fleet responsible for keeping down the Saxon and Frankish pirates. This man, a certain Carausius from what is now Holland, removed himself and his entire fleet to the British side of the Channel, where, as Roman commanders were apt to do, he assumed the title of emperor. For six years – such was the condition of the Empire – he was left in unchallenged control not only of the island but of the Gallic coast opposite. London found itself, however unenthusiastically, the capital of a virtually independent state.

Then, in 293, Carausius was assassinated by his own finance minister, Allectus, who took over the imperial title he had usurped. Rome was not prepared, however, to let this situation continue. In 296 Constantius Chlorus was sent over to deal with Allectus, who was soon defeated and killed. Constantius marched into London and overwhelmed the last of the rebels in the streets. A victory medal was struck, hailing him as 'Restorer of the eternal light'. Just ten years later, when he died in York, it was his son, the future Constantine the Great, who was in turn proclaimed emperor by the troops. Constantine marched south to make good his claim at the gates of Rome. That road of destiny presumably took him through London, where soon the mint was producing coins that bore his name. It was only on the coins, however, that London ever saw his face again.

The last century of Roman rule was increasingly darkened by the threat of barbarian invasion. The Picts and Scots might be far away in the north, but the Saxon and Frankish pirates were uncomfortably close. In 367 they overran the south-eastern coastal defences and ravaged the countryside up to the walls of London, which they blockaded. Fortunately help came from the Continent. The city was relieved by an army under Theodosius, father of the future Emperor Theodosius the Great.

By now, however, other barbaric hordes were battering at the frontiers of the Empire and it was Britain's turn to contribute forces elsewhere. Some of the garrison were drafted away in 401 or 402 to fight the Goths. Then, during the winter of 406, the Rhine froze hard from bank to bank, and in one night of epic disaster the barbarians were able to surge across the ice and pierce the imperial defences. It was like the bursting of a dam. The invaders flooded over Gaul and the last legionaries in Britain had to be shipped across in a vain effort to stem the tide. The fall of Rome itself came only four years afterwards. In that fatal year, 410, an urgent appeal went from Britain to the Emperor Honorius in his safe refuge among the Ravenna lagoons, begging for the return of at least some military forces. The feckless and distracted ruler could answer only that for the future the island must be responsible for its own protection.

The Roman age in Britain was at an end.

Honor salus et gloria Romanorum – 'the honour, welfare and glory of the Romans': victory medal of Constantius, after stamping out the breakaway movement of Allectus, AD 296.

2

The English and the Danes

Historic landmarks are not always recognized by the people living at the time. Yet in 410 nobody could have been in much doubt when news spread that Alaric and his Goths had set up their bivouacs in the squares of Rome. The world groaned, declared the North African St Augustine, and St Jerome in his monastic cell at Bethlehem wrote: 'The human race is included in the ruins.' In London, at the other extremity of the Empire, consternation can have been no less.

Despite the cataclysm, life went on. Alaric soon marched his horde away. The eternal city, though humiliated and diminished, survived. So in its smaller and less dramatic way did London. No exultant barbarians had appeared within its gates or even as yet been sighted from its walls. However threatening and disruptive the Saxon sea raids, it was to be another thirty-nine years, a lifetime for most people, before the Jutish chieftains Hengist and Horsa began the permanent conquest of the south-east.

For that period, and longer, the British carried on in London as best they could. If it was not quite 'business as usual', it was business as it had been for some time past. Trade had been diminishing as the economic difficulties of the Empire increased and the once-safe trade routes were threatened by civil war, barbarian incursions and general anarchy. Outlying provinces like Britain were not necessarily the worse for the change. They were largely self-sufficient except in the Mediterranean luxuries desired by the few – Britain, for example, was a grain-producer and the islanders lacked neither bread nor beer. For London itself, however, the import and export trade was vital. Long before independence was thrust upon the province, life in the city was running down like an unwound clock. Now, with the Cripplegate barracks empty of soldiers, with no colonial administrators or treasury officials, and with nothing to attract foreign merchants, the vital tick grew more hesitant. Even the native British population must have declined as men drifted away in search of a livelihood. From being a port busy with overseas trade and a provincial centre with a prosperous upper class, London became more of a market town dealing in foodstuffs, everyday commodities – and slaves. It was to this town, still protected by its Roman walls, that the British refugees flocked from Kent, the Anglo-Saxon Chronicle tells us, when Hengist drove them from their homes in 457, eight years after his landing.

After that date the historian is faced with a gap of almost a century and a half. There are no documents, and archaeological material is of the slightest. When London appears again in the Anglo-Saxon Chronicle (as 'Lunde-neric') in the year 604 it is a Saxon town, subject to the petty King of Essex. How did it become so? When did it cease to be British? Was it stormed, or

Opposite Viking horseman: detail from a Norwegian tapestry. Though best remembered for their long-ships, the Vikings were swift to commandeer horses and turn themselves at need into mounted infantry.

did the last of the original townsmen evacuate it, not merely in fear of the invaders but because it had become a ghost town in which there was no livelihood? Did the East Saxons at once move in, or did they shun the strangeness of those stone walls and paved streets, preferring to make their own settlements in clearings of the forest?

Opinion nowadays inclines to the view that London was never completely deserted, and that some Saxons were ready to use the site though they had not the skills to maintain the masonry and brickwork, the tiles and concrete, and the drains. Fresh light was shed by the excavations at Billingsgate in 1973, revealing a waterfront revetment of silver birch stakes, carbon-dated to about AD 760. As to the bridge, there is no means of knowing how long the Roman construction held together, or what efforts, if any, the Saxons made to patch up the inevitable wounds of time and weather. Late in the period – in the tenth century – there was certainly a timber bridge. The first documentary evidence is incidental and rather macabre, for it simply records that an unfortunate woman, suspected of witchcraft, was thrown off the bridge to drown. When this Saxon bridge was built, whether it was the first replacement of the Roman one, and for how long the Londoners had to rely on fords and ferries, are questions likely to baffle the historian indefinitely.

Whatever the precise date and manner of the English occupation of Romano-British London, the invaders could not have lost much time in establishing other settlements that today are as truly 'London' as the traditional City. Tooting was probably one such, as early as the fifth century. Wherever farming was possible – and we know that even prehistoric man had occupied sites in places such as Kensington and Wimbledon – the newcomers were soon turning their swords into ploughshares. Within a few generations the area round the original city was thickly dotted with such settlements. These, the villages and townships of later centuries, are the suburbs that eventually coalesced into the Greater London of our own day. By the eighth century most of them were already in existence and bearing names that we can still recognize.

In 604 London emerged from this twilight of uncertainty. A few years earlier that other St Augustine had arrived in Kent on his mission to convert England. London must by this time have made a considerable recovery, for Pope Gregory I suggested that Augustine make it his base. Circumstances decided otherwise. Augustine had to start his work at Canterbury, where the King of Kent's Frankish wife was already a Christian. King Ethelbert himself was gradually converted. Sebert, the lesser ruler of the East Saxons, was Ethelbert's nephew and acknowledged him as overlord. So, although London lay within the kingdom of Essex, the King of Kent had a royal residence within its walls, probably inside the perimeter of the old Roman fort at Cripplegate, an obvious enough place to choose. Sebert accepted his uncle and aunt's Christianity, and it was in 604 that Augustine consecrated one of his lieutenants, Mellitus, as Bishop of London. At the same time Ethelbert endowed the first cathedral church of St Paul and building began. Canterbury, however, had already been designated three years earlier as an archbishopric. Had matters gone more smoothly, the Pope's original intention might still have been fulfilled, and Canterbury might have lost to London

the primacy which it was in fact to retain ever afterwards. Any such plan was frustrated by Sebert's death in 616. His sons were still heathen, as were most of the Londoners. They drove Mellitus from his see. Ethelbert died about the same time, so there was no help from that quarter: with Ethelbert's death the Kentish supremacy faded. Augustine had been dead for several years.

For the next forty years London reverted to paganism. It is significant that foreign trade, now reviving, was mainly with the pagan Frisians across the North Sea. In 656 Christianity returned. This time it came from the north, for, with the decline of the Kentish influence, Essex – and consequently London – had come under the aegis of Northumbria. It was Finan, the Northumbrian bishop, who converted King Sigebert of Essex, and Finan who consecrated a new bishop for the long-vacant London see. He chose Cedda, brother of St Chad of Lichfield. From this date the line of London bishops runs continuous.

Outstanding among them was the fourth, Eorcenwald, who was appointed in 675 and died in 693. He was equally energetic, whether riding through the forests that still came close to the city walls and searching out remote hamlets where heathen superstition survived, or pressing forward with the improvement of his cathedral, where he would later be buried and his shrine venerated until the Reformation. His efforts were commemorated by a poem in his honour about 1386:

> Many a merry mason was made there to work,
> Hard stones for to hew with edged tools . . .

In the post-Roman twilight of the fifth and sixth centuries, the Saxon invaders beat their swords into ploughshares, or into the crude sickles, hoes and rakes of this later illustration (from a twelfth-century Pentateuch).

19

Nor did his building schemes stop at St Paul's. He founded an abbey at Chertsey and another at Barking, which was one of the great monasteries of the Anglo-Saxon period. It was mixed, as was quite common, but always headed by an abbess, the first being his own sister, Ethelburga. Barking Abbey had substantial endowments and influence in London: we hear at a later date of twenty-eight houses in the city owned by the abbess, and presumably let to tenants. One of London's oldest churches, close to the Tower, is significantly named All Hallows Barking. It dates from about 675 as a foundation – like all London's Saxon churches, the original building vanished long ago – and the living was in the Abbey's gift.

A very different city is now coming into view, a Christian city which has re-established links with the main culture of Europe and is becoming again, as in Roman times, a centre for foreign trade, even though, despite the new religion, that trade includes a brisk traffic in slaves. Anglo-Saxon England is moving into that golden age on which Alfred the Great, in the troubled ninth century, would look back as a paradise lost. 'It has often come into my remembrance,' he was to write to the Bishop of Worcester, 'what wise men there formerly were among the English race, and how foreigners came to this land for wisdom and instruction.'

London was not perhaps the place in which Anglo-Saxon culture and scholarship flowered conspicuously, but it provided a material basis. Bede, who died in 735, spoke of its commercial prosperity in his day. A century later, in 839, Bishop Helmstan of Winchester wrote of his recent consecration 'in the illustrious place, built by the skill of the ancient Romans, called throughout the world the great city of London'.

By this time its wealth became an attraction to the Vikings. In that same year they raided the city and were beaten off only when they had burnt and looted a number of houses and inflicted heavy casualties on the defenders. In 851 they came back with a bigger fleet. Three hundred and fifty longships came up the Thames and disgorged their ferocious crews. This host actually overran the city and burnt it down, an easy task when the buildings were so largely of wood and thatch. In 872 the invaders returned, and, instead of destroying the new houses, occupied them as winter quarters. Mercia, the

A relief on a runestone in a Gotland churchyard shows a Viking long-ship of the type that terrorized ninth-century London.

Ħ. dccclxxi· Her com reþere herea

ðingum onpefrearce· 7þær ymbe· iii· niht ridon

trezen eorlar up· þa ge mette æþel pulf ealdor

man hie oncængla felda· 7him þær pið zefeaht·

7rigenam 7heora peard oþer þær offlæzen

þær nama par Sidrac· Ða ymb· iiii· niht æþered

Extract from the Anglo-Saxon Chronicle, dealing with Alfred's 'year of battles' in 871.

The Anglo-Saxon kingdom of Mercia, spreading south and absorbing London, had cultural connections with the Continent. This illustration from a Saxon psalter ('Let the assembly of the peoples surround you; above them on high be enthroned') is copied from a Carolingian original.

Anglo-Saxon kingdom which had now spread southwards and absorbed London, was powerless to help.

It was Alfred of Wessex who liberated the city from these Danes. The peace he made with the defeated Guthrum in 886 drew the boundary of the Danelaw just east of London and restored the city to Mercia. Alfred handed it over to the alderman of Mercia, Ethelred, who had become his son-in-law by marrying Ethelfleda, but he maintained a keen personal interest and saw that the old walls were repaired and the defences looked to in every way. Alfred believed in strong towns as bulwarks against the assaults of his mobile enemies, and a strong London was central to his strategy. It was soon justified. In 896 a Danish fleet sailed up-river again, but the Londoners blocked its passage, sallied forth *en masse*, and after destroying some of the longships brought the best craft triumphantly back to the city.

Thereafter, for the best part of a hundred years, London stood strong and safe. In size and prosperity its pre-eminence was undeniable. Rather curiously, however, it was still not given the status of a capital. When the kings of Wessex found Winchester inconvenient for their coronation they used Kingston in preference to London, little more than ten miles away. Kingston, too, was the venue for the great ecclesiastical council summoned in 838. Earlier, the village of Chelsea – afterwards destroyed by the Danes – had been favoured for church synods. London itself remained, almost obstinately, the merchants' city. By the tenth century, though, the kings were increasingly calling their councils there. Great thanes and bishops found it worth while to have a town house to lodge them when they came on this or other business.

Evil days returned again under the weak rule of Ethelred the Unready, as he is inevitably remembered despite countless explanations that his nickname signifies 'without counsel' or 'ill-advised'. A great fire, apparently accidental, destroyed London in 981. It must have been rebuilt with the usual promptitude – not surprisingly, with the forest near at hand – for in the following year there was plenty for the Danes to burn down again when they attacked. Now the Londoners were back in the perilous atmosphere their forefathers had known before their deliverance by Alfred.

In 994 there was a combined Scandinavian attack. Olaf Tryggvason, then an exile from Norway, allied with Swein, the similarly exiled King of Denmark, assailed London Bridge with nearly a hundred ships, probably manned by Swedish Vikings from Russia, where Olaf himself had spent his boyhood at Novgorod. On this occasion the raiders were repelled, but in the end Ethelred had to buy them off. Olaf kept his bargain and never returned, but the Danes came back to England again and again, while Ethelred made futile efforts to appease them. London stood firm. In 1009 a chronicler wrote, 'Praise be to God, it stands yet untouched, and always they suffer loss there.' But now Swein, who had long ago recovered his Danish kingdom, determined to be King of England as well. Town after town submitted to him, till he was almost universally acknowledged, but London withstood him until Ethelred had decamped to safety in Normandy and there seemed little point in remaining loyal to so inadequate a ruler. London surrendered and for a spell the Danes held the city. But very soon, in February 1014, Swein himself died at Gainsborough. The thanes and principal churchmen, assembled in the Witan to express the national will, invited Ethelred to return, on his solemn promise to do better in the future.

Carved wooden comb with Viking-style decoration, found underneath Cheapside.

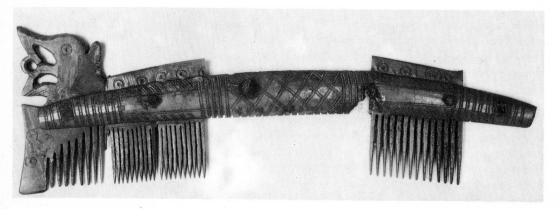

A page from an eleventh-century Anglo-Saxon MS. shows a Viking battle-scene.

Swein had left a formidable successor in his son, Canute, though for the moment Canute sailed away and avoided conflict. London, however, had to be cleared of its Danish garrison. Luckily Ethelred had the help of another Norwegian Olaf, Olaf Haraldsson, later to become St Olaf but at this date a nineteen-year-old adventurer, very willing to fight for the English against the Danes. It was he who, at the sixth attempt, succeeded in breaching the barrier formed by London Bridge. His ships wound cables round the timbers supporting it and then were rowed hard downstream until their combined power dislodged some of the posts and caused a section of the bridge to collapse. This was the episode preserved in folk memory by the old rhyme, 'London Bridge is falling down . . .' With it collapsed the resistance of the Danes and the city returned to English control.

The restored king did not live long. Ethelred died in 1016, and London was quickly involved in the armed struggle for the succession. The majority of the Witan, gathered in Southampton, offered the crown to Canute. The remainder, meeting in London, stood by the son of Ethelred by his first marriage, the splendid and well-named warrior Edmund Ironside. Twice Canute besieged London, twice Edmund marched up from the West Country and relieved the city. It was during one of these sieges that Canute, anxious to complete his blockade and frustrated as usual by the barrier of London Bridge, quite literally got round the difficulty by having a ditch dug round the southern bridgehead, at Southwark, so that some of his ships could be hauled across and launched in the upper reaches of the stream. Who would have eventually won this ding-dong war for mastery can never be known, for after six months Edmund died, whether naturally or by foul play, and there was then no one to challenge Canute. Ethelred's widow, his second wife, Emma, clinched the matter by marrying him.

Bone gaming counter of Viking origin, found in London.

King Canute, promoter of London's prosperity, with Queen Emma, mother of Edward the Confessor.

The Battle of Hastings was now just fifty years away. The complexities of that last half-century of Anglo-Saxon England – Anglo-Danish would be a truer description – may be clarified if a few personal relationships are borne in mind. Emma was herself the daughter of the then Duke of Normandy, so that her son by Ethelred, Edward the Confessor, was half Norman by blood and even more so by upbringing. By Canute she had another son, Hardi-canute, who ruled briefly and cruelly after his father's death. But London's history over this period falls into two main parts, the reign of Canute, when Danish enterprise built up the trading prosperity of the city to a new level, and the reign of Edward, marked by the permeation of Norman influences long before the military victory of William over Harold.

London had now a population of at least twelve thousand, much less than its peak in Roman times but considerable for that period. Every citizen was free to attend the great folk moot, held on the open hilltop close to St Paul's. Civil and commercial disputes were thrashed out in the 'husting', a weekly court presided over by the aldermen, the archaic name of which continued into the days of Lord Mayors and Guildhall. The city was divided into wards, each with its lesser court for petty cases, conducted by one of these same aldermen. One has an impression, quite different from that of Romano-British London, of a lively, independent-minded population, in which individuals spoke out and the city as a whole was not slow to assert itself in

puteū q̄ oſtenderat dc̄s agar. quē foderat abrahā. ante
n. ⁊ ſerui abimeleċ abſtulerant illum abrahe. ⁊ reſtituit ei abi
leċ puteū·

Inege hyp

national affairs. This impression is reinforced by the extreme delicacy, not to say deference, with which William handled the Londoners even after his conclusive triumph at Hastings. History had already shown that the city was not easy to blockade if its inhabitants were resolute in resistance. Nor, faced with so much manpower, was any general ever again to welcome any plan of attack that would involve street-fighting. Add the impressive economic strength of London even in those days – at Canute's accession it paid one-eighth of the tribute collected from the whole of England – and one realizes that London had by this time consolidated its unique position. As was to be demonstrated all down the Middle Ages and by the Civil War itself, no contender for power stood much chance unless he commanded the loyalty of the Londoners.

Canute's eighteen-year reign brought peace and prosperity to a city that must have been weary of manning its walls. The Danes themselves were notable traders with useful connections all over northern Europe. There had been Danes living in London before, until the massacre Ethelred so ill-advisedly ordered on St Brice's Day in 1002, but now the Danish merchants could return with confidence under a king of their own nationality. Many settled on the vacant ground just west of the gates, where the name Aldwych and the church of St Clement Danes point to their former presence. It was usual for foreign merchants, and newcomers in general, to form close-knit

Saxon king and council.

The first Westminster Abbey coronation: Harold, as depicted on the Bayeux Tapestry.

Coin of Edward the Confessor.

communities for mutual protection. There were Frenchmen, Germans and other aliens. An old document which may date from Ethelred's time or Canute's, governing the various tolls payable by ships at Billingsgate, mentions 'men from Rouen', 'men from Flanders and Ponthieu and Normandy and the Isle of France', 'men from Huy and Liège and Nivelles', and 'subjects of the Emperor', while the commodities include wine, fish, timber and cloth as well as smaller items such as gloves and pepper.

London's international importance was even more enhanced by Canute's supremacy in northern Europe. He was King not only of England but of Denmark, and then by conquest of Norway too. He chose England by preference as his headquarters, promising to rule the English according to their old laws. Had his brief empire held together after his death, London could have been the capital of an Anglo-Scandinavian state encircling the North Sea. It was not to be. Canute could not command the tide, as he demonstrated to his sycophantic courtiers in that famous incident which traditionally took place on the bank of the Thames at Lambeth. Nor could he determine events once his own firm hand was removed and his sons were left to squabble over his legacy.

Those squabbles ended, Edward the Confessor was raised to the throne in 1042, in theory restoring the old English line but in practice paving the way to the Norman Conquest. Within two years Edward had appointed a Norman as Bishop of London, that Robert of Jumièges whom in due course he promoted, most controversially, to the archbishopric of Canterbury.

Edward's more lasting contribution to London life was Westminster Abbey. More than three centuries earlier there had been Benedictine monks settled on what was then Thorney Island in the Thames. Subsequently, the place had been used as a royal residence. Canute had held court there with his bodyguard of house-carles. Edward had made it his favourite home. What really absorbed him was the dream of restoring, far more splendidly, the ancient monastery, and he put this work in hand soon after he became King. He lived just long enough to see the abbey church consecrated, over twenty years afterwards, on 28 December 1065. That building, long vanished, was significantly in the Norman style he so much admired. On 5 January he died, and was buried in his new church the following day. He left no son, and his nearest kinsman was his great-nephew, Edgar Atheling, a child hardly competent to rule England in that disturbed period. In any case, there was still no rigid rule of succession. Not surprisingly, therefore, Edgar was passed over. With his dying breath Edward nominated Harold, Earl of Wessex, as his successor. Harold had some royal blood and for years past had been virtually governing the country in Edward's name. The decision lay with the Witan, and that assembly endorsed the choice of Harold, who was quickly crowned in the abbey, thereby starting the tradition which Edward had expressly wished to establish in that place.

So opened the fateful year of 1066. Before it ended, on Christmas Day to be precise, there had been a second coronation, that of William the Conqueror.

Coins of Harold (*top*) and William the Conqueror.

27

Ste Wille det Bastardus diir Normanos angham sibi expulso Rege haraldo triumphato magnificus potent Adquisita sub iugau Abbacia de bello ubi tumpharat fundau. Regnau anis xvi. z aplus

Iste Wilts. Rufus dictus z cristens anglos nobiles eques pa trem ei recepert z ipm tauert insepis fatigau z expulir Aula Westm ostrut. tande sagta piit fiem regnauit Ams xii.

Willelm ner anglie priipco equsiconem ei

Willem nere sede Rufus

Henricus se nos ker sci an ano co

Stephii ker pri an co co

Iste henricus vir potens z sapiens Jurati leges sci edmardi in ci abitit tene. h fiem uicat frem suii: noluit. Nobile cenobii de Radigo ubi sepult iac: fundau. z epatu ostruit kik. Regnau aii arniis xxxvii: z ereiter dimidiii. an co co co

Iste Stephanus miles strenuissinii omnib; diebz dubiis casibz bellox intistnit. Isto Abbaciam de fenrcham fundaut. In qua ipe z eustachii sihiis cei z awaldis regna turen ei iacent sepulti. Iste Regnauit Anni. s. xiv.

3

The Town Fitzstephen Knew

Those ten autumn weeks between Hastings and the coronation saw much anguished debate among the Londoners.

The lost battle and the fallen King did not seem, as they seem to us with hindsight, historically decisive. The Normans, though formidable, were few. London had defied other invaders, and the first instinct was to defy William too. Encouraged by both archbishops and the great northern earls, the Londoners proclaimed their new king to be the boy Edgar Atheling, grandson of that Edmund Ironside they had backed against Canute. When the Norman knights rode into Southwark, they found London Bridge closed against them. William made no suicidal attempt to force the crossing. He continued his march up-river on the Surrey side. Looking across the water, the townspeople saw the sky redden as Southwark went up in flames. That had happened before. Frustrated attackers usually vented their feelings on hapless Southwark.

William crossed the Thames at Wallingford. The steel snake of mail-clad riders twisted back towards London. Doubts began to multiply in the city. If England had still possessed an undisputed, unifying leader there would have been good prospects for resistance. So big a walled city would have been hard to besiege with so small an army, and the Duke would scarcely have fancied street-fighting in which his mounted men would have lost all their advantage against the Saxon axes. But Edgar Atheling could not fill the role of Harold, the northern earls had retired to their own distant domains, and the flower of the southern fighting men had died at Hastings. A chilly breath of isolation blew through London. The red sky over Southwark might be the portent of worse weather ahead: William's progress had been marked by a deliberate policy of terror. Finally, as the faint-hearted – or the prudent and law-respecting? – could argue, the Duke had quite a persuasive set of arguments supporting his claim to the throne. So there was a revision of policy. A delegation rode out to meet William at Berkhamsted. They found the terrible man sweetly reasonable. He had no intention of upsetting the laws they had observed in King Edward's day. All their old rights and privileges would be guaranteed. Property would be respected. 'I will that every child be his father's heir,' promised William, 'and I will not endure that any man offer wrong to you.'

They then invited him to enter London in peace, which he did with great ceremony, the aldermen meeting him at the gates and surrendering the keys. Then, in due course, he went to Westminster for coronation in traditional form. When the knights on guard outside the abbey heard the thunderous

Opposite The four Norman kings: William I, William Rufus, Henry I and Stephen.

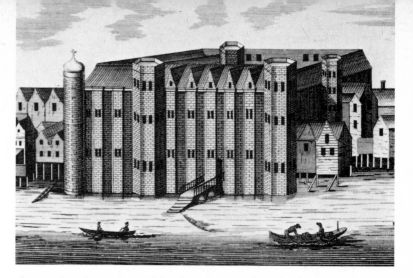

Baynard's Castle, built by Ralph Baynard on the Thames at Blackfriars.

shouts of acclamation within, they thought there had been a treacherous attack upon their leader, and, as a reprisal, they set fire to the homes of the innocent people of Westminster. So, though London itself was unharmed by the events of 1066, both the main towns outside its boundary suffered badly.

The city was not to see much of its new King. Most of William's reign was spent on distant campaigns in England, Wales, Scotland, or on the Continent, where he died. He pleased Londoners by giving them their writs and charters in English. Everyday life was probably less affected among the trading community than in the landowning class and the upper ranks of the clergy, where the old notables were quickly displaced by Normans. There were, however, one or two significant appointments within the city. Thus the command of the 'host', the mass levy of able-bodied men in time of emergency, was now given to one of the Duke's followers, Ralph Baynard, who built himself a massive fortress, Baynard's Castle, on the riverside at what is now Blackfriars. A later Baynard, in the fourteenth century, gave his name to Bayswater.

Baynard's Castle was not the only Norman stronghold rising within the city. Close by was another, Montfichet, its exact site now unknown. And down-river in the south-east corner, destined to stand long after the other two had been demolished, was the Tower. It began as the usual early Norman defence-work, an earth mound inside a ditch. Then William called on the architectural skill of Gundulf, nicknamed 'the weeping monk of Bec', who had been made Bishop of Rochester and was rebuilding the ruined Saxon cathedral there. Thenceforth Gundulf had to spend much of his time in London. The great square keep was started, afterwards to be known as the White Tower from the coating of whitewash it was given. The work went slowly, not helped by a phenomenal gale in 1090, which blew down all the scaffolding – not surprisingly, since it also flattened more than six hundred wooden houses in the city. The building was not completed until about 1100, the year Henry I succeeded William Rufus as King, but if Gundulf's work was slow it was also sure. The White Tower he saw in his old age is substantially the one we see today, apart from the altered windows and other details that date from Christopher Wren's restoration.

Opposite St John's Chapel, in the White Tower – London's oldest place of worship.

If Baynard commanded the London host, the Constable of the Tower, a de Mandeville, held the right to raise men from a wide tract of country outside the walls – what in modern times became the East End, Bethnal Green, Stepney, Limehouse, and all the other districts as far as Chaucer's 'Stratford-atte-Bowe'. Stepney figures in the Domesday survey as 'Stevenhethe', a hythe or haven on the river just below the city.

All round London lay other villages and hamlets, some also mentioned in Domesday, such as Islington and St Pancras. Marylebone was then called Tyburn, from the stream that flowed down towards Westminster, forking to make the island on which the abbey stood. Besides the old Saxon settlements new ones sprang up, often connected with the religious houses which the zealous Normans endowed. At Bermondsey, just south of Southwark, a Cluniac priory was established in 1087, which developed into a wealthy abbey in its own right and inevitably gathered a lay population round its walls. At the other end of the scale, Kilburn began in the twelfth century as a tiny offshoot of Westminster, just three nuns and a chaplain, but as all the ladies were former maids of honour to Henry I's queen their social connections doubtless made up for their scanty numbers.

Of all these peripheral settlements Westminster continued far the most important, retaining the royal status it had acquired before the Conquest. The Norman kings might value the Tower as a means of dominating London, but they preferred the Palace of Westminster as their own residence. Rufus rebuilt the palace in 1097. The great hall survives from that date, or at least its lower walls do: the splendid timber roof, one of the largest in Europe, was made for Richard II by his carpenter, Hugh Herland, at the end of the fourteenth century.

By degrees the picture of London familiar to modern eyes begins to appear – or, if not a picture, a ground plan. We have an abbey, a cathedral at St Paul's, a Thames bridge, though none of them yet in its present form. We have the White Tower, however, at one end and Westminster Hall at the other, both still extant, and one or two other landmarks that survive today. The Knights Templars came to London in 1118, first to Chancery Lane, then removing to the Temple, where the round nave and west door of their church remain from its original consecration in 1185. Even older, indeed the oldest church in the city if we exclude the chapel in the White Tower, is the chancel of St Bartholomew's, a relic of the Augustinian priory and hospital which Henry I's courtier, Rahere, established in 1123.

Luckily we have an animated description of life in Norman London preserved for us by a contemporary writer, William Fitzstephen. Fitzstephen was Becket's chaplain and a horrified eyewitness of the Canterbury tragedy. What more natural than that he should be the one to write Becket's biography, four years after the murder and immediately after his master's canonization? Becket was a Londoner, Fitzstephen was another – and obviously proud of it. He, therefore, prefaced his book with an enthusiastic word-picture of the city, which, while not particularly relevant to his theme, has left us a priceless document on early social life which is the envy of other European capitals.

Fitzstephen wrote in 1174. He sketches in the general picture from the Tower westwards to 'the royal palace' at Westminster, 'an incomparable

A thumbnail sketch of London, from an itinerary by the thirteenth-century historian, Matthew Paris, shows the wall, St Paul's and the 'Tamise' beyond.

St Thomas à Becket, a Londoner of Norman parentage: a pilgrim's badge found in the Thames at Dowgate.

structure, furnished with a breastwork and bastions, situated in a populous suburb'. He counts up to thirteen 'larger conventual churches' and 'one hundred and thirty-six lesser parochial ones'. He makes flattering and prob-ably debatable generalizations about the manners and morals of the citizens, and of the married women observes merely that they 'are perfect Sabines'. 'The only inconveniences of London', he says, 'are the immoderate drinking of foolish persons and the frequent fires.' The latter were inevitable so long as thatch and timber were the common building materials. There had been two great conflagrations in early Norman times, in August 1077 'such a one' (recorded the Anglo-Saxon Chronicle) 'as never was before since London was founded', and a second only ten years later which destroyed St Paul's and 'the greatest and fairest part of the whole city'. There was a third disaster in 1136, of which Fitzstephen may have retained youthful memories: this fire raged from Aldgate and London Bridge to St Paul's, where it burnt the new nave then under construction and destroyed the shrine of St Eorcenwald, though the saint's relics were carried to safety by a Norman soldier. Fitz-stephen must have highly approved the law passed towards the end of his life (it followed Richard I's accession in 1189) which required that the lower storey at least of a new house should be built of stone and that thatching should give place to roofs of tile or slate.

A pilgrim's badge found in the City.

Si menrai auoec moi mon neueu gadifier

A glimpse of the school-life so vividly described by Fitzstephen.

Craftsmen painters at work: illumination in the twelfth-century Dover Bible.

The charm and full value of Fitzstephen's account emerge only when he has dutifully given us his few facts and figures, paid the expected but meaningless compliments, and feels free to indulge in personal impressions and nostalgia. 'For we have all been boys', he remarks in a wistful parenthesis, and there is certainly a youthful emphasis in his series of vignettes. Through his eyes we see the London year revolve, starting with Shrovetide, when 'the boys of the respective schools' – at St Paul's, that was, and St Martin's-le-Grand, and Stratford-at-Bow – 'bring each a fighting cock to their master, and the whole of that forenoon is spent by the boys in seeing their cocks fight in the school-room.' After dinner, there was football – 'the well-known game of foot-ball' – in the fields outside the city. 'The scholars belonging to the several schools have each their ball; and the city tradesmen, according to their respective crafts, have theirs.' The parents rode out to watch, and, like parents of later generations, 'their natural heat aroused by the sight of so much agility', were often tempted into 'participation in the amusements of unrestrained youth'. 'After their manner' is Fitzstephen's qualification, as if to remind us that this is forty years on.

Then, throughout Lent, each Sunday afternoon saw horse-races and sham fights in those same fields, while the Easter holidays drew crowds to the river to witness 'a game resembling a naval engagement', though it was more like an aquatic tournament, for it involved a young man with a lance, standing in the prow of a boat and tilting at a target fixed to a tree-trunk in midstream. It would be about this time of year too, presumably, that the townspeople would begin to enjoy 'dramatic performances' representing miracles or the

King John hunting a stag.
Citizens too enjoyed sporting
rights in the 'immense forest'
close by.

sufferings of the martyrs. These were staged at places like Clerkenwell, just outside the walls.

The summer evenings brought the young men out for 'the sports of leaping, archery, wrestling, stone-throwing, slinging javelins beyond a mark, and also fighting with bucklers'. Nor did Fitzstephen fail to mention 'the dances of the maidens, who merrily trip along the ground beneath the uprisen moon'. One senses in his writing a particular affection for the countryside that stretched between the last houses and the fringe of the greenwood, where the young people 'go out to take the air in the summer evenings'. There were fields of pasture on the north side of the city, 'and a delightful plain of meadow land, interspersed with flowing streams, on which stand mills, whose clack is very pleasing to the ear. Close by lies an immense forest, in which are densely wooded thickets, the coverts of game, stags, fallow-deer, boars, and wild bulls.' The citizens, he says, had wide hunting rights, all over the Chilterns and south-eastwards into Kent. Most of them 'amuse themselves in sporting with merlins, hawks, and other birds . . . and also with dogs that hunt in the woods.'

With autumn and winter came bull-baiting, and, if a really cold snap came, there would be skating on Moorfields, 'that great marsh which washes the walls of the city on the north side'. In one of his best-known passages he describes how

the young men go out in crowds to divert themselves upon the ice. Some, having increased their velocity by a run, placing their feet apart, and turning their bodies

Bear-baiting was a popular sport in medieval London.

sideways, slide a great way. Others make a seat of large pieces of ice like mill-stones, and a great number of them running before, and holding each other by the hand, draw one of their companions who is seated on the ice. If at any time they slip in moving so swiftly, all fall down headlong together. Others are more expert in their sports upon the ice. For fitting to, and binding under their feet the shinbones of some animal, and taking in their hands poles shod with iron, which at times they strike against the ice, they are carried along with as great rapidity as a bird flying or a bolt discharged from a crossbow.

Other passages are equally vivid. There is an account of the horse-fairs, with their accompanying races and displays, held every Friday on 'a certain smooth field' we now call Smithfield. And there is an enthusiastic description of a public eating-house down by the river where 'every day, according to the season, may be found viands of all kinds, roast, fried and boiled, fish large and small, coarser meat for the poor, and more delicate for the rich, such as venison, fowls, and small birds.' It reads as though take-away meals were supplied, for, 'if friends, wearied with their journey, should unexpectedly come to a citizen's house, and, being hungry, should not like to wait till fresh meat be bought and cooked, some run to the river side, and there everything that they could wish for is instantly procured.'

It is noticeable that Fitzstephen is silent on the subject of London Bridge. At the time when he was writing there was good reason for this omission.

Peter de Colechurch, a fellow cleric, had been given the task eleven years previously of replacing the bridge lost in the fire of 1136. Between that date and 1163 people had presumably made do with a ferry, just as, for a period prior to 1120, they had been without the earlier bridge swept away by a gale. Fitzstephen may well have felt that this was not a feature of London to dwell upon, but he may also have been genuinely uncertain about the future. Peter de Colechurch had just built what was to be the last of the London Bridges made of timber. Whether he intended it all along to be only a temporary structure, or whether he simply felt dissatisfied with it, he went on to the project of a stone bridge, destined to serve until the early nineteenth century. Fitzstephen may have known of this idea as he wrote in 1174, for in 1176 the stone construction was actually begun, parallel with the timber erection already in use.

Wrestling – one of the many pastimes mentioned by Fitzstephen.

It was an ambitious project, difficult, dangerous and costly. It took thirty years and is said to have cost 150 lives. Henry II helped to finance it with a tax on wool, and the Church made substantial contributions.

To build piers of masonry in a tidal river was obviously more of a technical problem than driving timbers into the bed of the stream. Piles had to be driven anyhow, and this could be done from barges, but the rest of the work below water level was not so straightforward. The Elizabethan historian, Stow, tells us that the course of the Thames was diverted between Battersea and Rotherhithe.

Twenty piers were built, supporting nineteen arches. The spacing was quite irregular and reflects the pragmatic approach of the medieval engineer. The piers went where it proved possible to get the piles in and to construct the masonry upon them. The piles were of elm. They were hammered into the river-bed in elliptical groups, palisade fashion, and then the centre was filled up with rubble, and stout beams of oak were laid horizontally across the top. This basic structure, known as a 'starling', was bigger than the actual pier which then sprang from it to carry the arch. All through the centuries of old London Bridge the starlings were to prove a menace to boat-men by still further narrowing the stream and turning each archway into a foaming mill-race when the tide was on the ebb.

These openings varied in width from thirty-four feet to as little as fifteen. The piers were more standardized. Colechurch made them usually about twenty feet wide, but in the middle, where he planned a chapel in memory of St Thomas, the pier measured thirty-five feet. The chapel projected down-stream and rested on an enlarged starling, which served as a landing-stage permitting fishermen and boatmen to enter direct from their craft, using a lower door. The chapel was not the only building on the bridge. There were shops and houses from the beginning, and their rents were sensibly allocated by King John to maintenance. The defensive aspect of the bridge was not forgotten. Crossing from Southwark one came, after two arches, to a great stone gate, massively fortified. Four further arches led to a drawbridge and another gate. The drawbridge was raised for tall-masted ships to pass through – on payment of sixpence. The chapel of St Thomas came after another four arches. When Colechurch died in 1205, his work still unfinished, he was buried in its crypt with the river he had conquered roaring past on either side.

Doubtless, and understandably, he may have been failing some years before that, or King John was growing impatient. At all events it was in 1202 that the King, after taking the advice of the Archbishop of Canterbury, called in a noted Frenchman, Isenbert, to help. As he explained to the Londoners, Isenbert had already built bridges at Saintes and Rochelle with commendable speed. Whatever the importance of his contribution, the bridge was completed at last in 1209. Stow makes no mention of Isenbert but names Serle Mercer, William Almaine and Benedict Botewrite as 'principal masters of that work'. The traders of Southwark were thereafter allowed to hold their market on the bridge. Traffic in those days had to be patient.

Even then, the troubles of the famous river-crossing were not over. In 1212 yet another great fire broke out, consuming an area at each end and destroying all the wooden buildings on it. In 1283 there was a hard winter and a great

Rogues and vagabonds: the pillory, no less than the prison cell, afforded facilities for meditation.

weight of ice piled up against the piers. Five arches were badly damaged, but the bridge as a whole stood firm. Peter de Colechurch had done his work well.

Another topic on which Fitzstephen is silent is the guilds, though they were becoming important in the life of the city. He mentions tradesmen only incidentally, in connection with the Shrovetide football.

The London guilds, now surviving ceremonially as the livery companies, named from the standard dress they adopted later in the Middle Ages, claim somewhat vague origins in Anglo-Saxon times. The *frith-gild* of those days, however, was more of a neighbourhood association for mutual protection and shared responsibility, and it was only because members of the same craft or trade tended to congregate in one locality that they came also to have common working interests. By Norman times these interests became para-mount. The social and insurance aspects remained – members of the same guild met for convivial functions, helped sick colleagues, and paid for the funerals and masses when they died – but the trade was the unifying factor. Soon, to earn a living, rich man and poor man alike had to belong to the appropriate merchant guild or craft guild, or work as apprentice or journey-man for someone who did.

Both the goldsmiths and the weavers had a London guild in the time of Henry I. His grandson, Henry II, gave the weavers a charter confirming their rights and excluding any non-member from plying the craft in the city or in Southwark or any of the other suburbs. For this protection the guild paid the King 1,440 silver pennies a year, which they soon increased to 1,600 when they were afraid of losing it. Such contributions to the royal revenue earned the guilds a position of considerable importance.

As the institutions of local government evolved, the guilds formed the natural channels through which power flowed. Even today, when the real administration of London is directed from County Hall across the river, Guildhall preserves, with all its historical ceremonies, the outline of what was for centuries the actual working system. The Lord Mayor and other officers are elected by the 'freemen' of the city, but these freemen qualify by membership of a livery company.

London's first charter was granted by Henry I in 1130. The aim of the citizens, like those of Lincoln at the same time, was to have direct access to the Crown, independently of the shire in which their town stood. As with the guilds, recognition had to be paid for. The Londoners gave the King a hundred silver marks for the right to choose their own sheriff, which meant, among other things, that they controlled the collection of their own taxes and paid them straight to the Exchequer. In practice they handed over an agreed round sum or 'farm', since the primitive system of that age could not address an individual buff envelope to every citizen. It is understandable why each closely knit town community was anxious to get this business into its own hands and out of those of some less sympathetic outsider such as the King's officer for the shire.

London did not see much of the Norman kings. They were seldom at Westminster. Much of their time was spent in France, and most of the rest on campaigns or progresses. Government was where the king was. But each

Loading a merchant ship.

ruler in turn betrayed his realization of the city's importance. After the distinctly mysterious demise of Rufus in the New Forest – an affair still unclarified, in which the finger of scholarly suspicion points increasingly at his younger brother, Henry – that same brother made for London with indecent speed. The alleged accident occurred one August evening. Henry at once rode twenty miles to Winchester to secure the royal treasury there, and before nine o'clock next morning was riding hard for London, seventy miles away, where he arrived at dusk. On the following day the Bishop of London was fetched to Westminster and a coronation performed. Henry wanted to secure his position without the loss of an hour, for his other brother, Robert, was on his way home from the crusade.

Henry I was the monarch who (as the old nursery histories used to teach) 'never smiled again' after the loss of his only son in the sinking of the *White Ship*. The consequence was that when he died in 1135 there was no clear successor. Should it be his daughter Matilda, or his nephew Stephen? Who

The king and parliament. Government, in the Middle Ages, was where the king was; the admonitory royal forefinger seems to symbolize the dominant role of the monarch.

had the first right, the daughter of the Conqueror's son or the son of the Conqueror's daughter? In the years of civil war that followed, the Londoners inclined to Stephen's side.

Matilda's arrogance did not go down with them. Betrothed at seven to the Holy Roman Emperor, she had been brought up in Germany from that age and her manners were Teutonic and imperious. Though widowed and since remarried to the Count of Anjou, she was still very much the Empress Matilda, and it was in that tone that she talked to the London notables when at last, in 1141, she took triumphant possession of their city. She had defeated her cousin, whom these insolent townsmen had ill-advisedly proclaimed king. He was her captive at Bristol, she had collected the crown at Winchester, and now she meant to have it placed on her head with due ceremony in Westminster Abbey.

That ceremony never took place. During the preparations she managed to offend everybody – and to forget that Stephen's wife was still at large with an unbeaten army not far away in Kent. With London on her side, she could have laughed at it. Instead, as she sat down to dinner that Midsummer Day in the Palace of Westminster, news came that London was in revolt and had opened its gates to Stephen's supporters. She had barely time to escape, riding at top speed with a small retinue to Oxford sixty miles away. She never re-captured London. The next coronation, when it came, was that of her son, Henry II, who on Stephen's death, succeeded under the compromise agreement already made.

Henry II tended to view London with a somewhat jaundiced eye. He never forgot its treatment of his mother, and, having spent most of his life on the Continent, he did not like what he had seen of independent cities. Under a weak or non-existent central government – as in the anarchic period of Stephen and Matilda – London might conceivably have developed like the communes of Europe. The strong, dynamic control of the first Plantagenet scotched any notion that it should go the way of the Flemish or Italian cities. He took away the civic privileges granted by his grandfather and increased the taxes. London did not regain the *status quo* until Henry was succeeded by Richard I, who was quite ready to barter municipal liberties to finance his real interest, a new crusade.

The Great Seal of Henry II, in whose reign Fitzstephen wrote his famous description of London life.

Though Richard did not often show his face in London, he provided a memorable coronation which served as the model for subsequent ceremonies. There were three days of festivity. Ladies were barred from the state banquets, but the clergy had honoured places. We may hope that Fitzstephen was able to participate in a programme he would certainly have enjoyed. The coronation was on 3 September 1189, and he seems to have been alive a year or two later.

Unfortunately the proceedings were marred by a tragic misunderstanding. Jews had been excluded from what Richard regarded as a Christian celebration, but some of their community appeared at the palace with suitable gifts. Refused admission, they were attacked by the bystanders. A pogrom began which Richard's officers, sent out to inquire the cause of the uproar, were powerless to control. The disorder spread through London. Numerous Jews were murdered and their homes looted.

It was during Richard's reign that London's first mayor was appointed, the city's spokesman having previously been known as the portreeve. Henry Fitzailwin took office in 1193, during the King's captivity in Austria. He was a natural civic leader, son and grandson of men prominent in London's affairs, and he remained mayor until his death in 1212. King John then laid it down in a new charter he granted in 1215, the same year as an even more famous charter, that in future the mayors should be elected annually. Fitzailwin's long supremacy illustrates a tendency, not unknown in later times, for local government to be dominated by an outstanding individual or a clique. In 1196 the poorer Londoners rose in arms against the regime of Fitzailwin and the twenty-four aldermen from the leading guilds associated with him. This riot was put down by the King's Justiciar, but when John came to power, though not a ruler noted for his democratic sympathies, he did try to provide for a more widely elected council, whose two dozen members were not restricted to aldermen. This change did not, however, last long.

John died in 1216 and was succeeded by his nine-year-old son as Henry III. With his eventful reign, lasting until 1272, a new chapter of London's history opens.

4

The Seat of Government

From the thirteenth century London is truly the capital of England, not merely the biggest and richest town, but the base for a more and more static, centralized administration, a true seat of government. Hitherto, government had been wherever the king happened to be, and justice similarly. Medieval kings toured continually. They had to, to maintain control and contact. For their own comfort they had to, being driven by the problems of catering for a vast entourage and by the mounting stench of their crude sanitary arrangements.

It may not be entirely without significance that Henry III, whose reign saw such a change in these nomadic habits and such a development in London's role as a capital, was also a man who took a keen personal interest in household details, both decorative and practical. These are well documented. He told the Constable of the Tower:

Since the privy chamber of our wardrobe is situated in an undue and improper place, wherefore it smells badly, we command you on the faith and love by which you are bounden unto us, that you in no wise omit to cause another privy chamber to be made in the same wardrobe in such more fitting and proper place as you may select there, even though it should cost a hundred pounds.

Henry's concern for such matters was stimulated and informed by his marriage to Eleanor of Provence, who brought with her many ideas from the cultured South, and set a fashion for fitted baths, glass windows, wainscoted walls and painted hangings. It was in this period that London got its first piped water supply, conveyed from the Tyburn stream.

It would be frivolous, of course, to imply that Henry's love of domestic comfort was a major factor in centralizing the government on London. Henry continued to tour his realm and the records show that he was quite capable of ensuring that comfort in any castle he planned to visit. He was a great builder and improver, but he did not confine his efforts to the Tower, which he turned from a comparatively small fortress into a massive concentric citadel, or to Westminster, where he rebuilt the entire abbey church much as we see it today, and carried out extensive alterations to the palace. Magnificent as these achievements were, and meticulous as was his attention to the details – we still know what he paid his clerk for the cherry-trees to be planted in his Westminster garden – they did not cause him to neglect Windsor or Nottingham or any of the other royal residences. Certainly Henry (though he did not particularly like the Londoners) made Westminster more of a settled home than his predecessors had done. His son, the first Edward, was born

Thirteenth-century seal of the city of London. St Paul presides over and protects the city, symbolized by walls, a gate, towers and church spires.

Opposite King Edward I and his parliament. From Edward's time, Westminster became the normal meeting-place.

43

sic collato memoria donatorus indelebi.   Willegodum. Qz interpretat volens bonu.

Top Henry III, an enthusiastic builder, instructs his masons during the complete reconstruction of Westminster Abbey.

Right The Abbey after its rebuilding. The essential design is unaltered today.

there, and he himself was to die there. But London's final crystallization as the seat of government depended on less personal causes.

That government was developing in complexity as the years went by. The sheer paperwork – or at first, to be more strictly accurate, the accumulation of parchment rolls and wooden tallies – made it impossible to run the country from an itinerant headquarters. The king must still travel, riding forth along unspeakable roads at the head of an endless creaking column of conscripted wagons, stuffed with everything from bedding and tapestries to Books of Hours and timbrels. But the complete apparatus of government, the embryo civil service, its accounts and other records, could no longer be dragged behind him.

Three departments were emerging: the Exchequer, under its Chancellor, then as now concerned with collecting revenue; the Chancery, an ever-expanding secretariat with control of the Great Seal; and finally the Wardrobe, with the Privy Seal, in theory dealing with the monarch's personal and household expenses. Demarcation was difficult. When refractory barons dominated the Chancery, a resourceful king could sometimes bypass their obstruction by channelling business through the Wardrobe accounts.

The routine work of all departments was increasingly transacted in London. True, wherever the king went, he must still take high officers and confidential clerks. But the day-to-day business could be carried on only in the capital. Similarly, to comply with a Magna Carta provision that 'common pleas shall not follow our court but shall be held in some fixed place', the law courts were established first in Westminster Hall itself and then near by, until the present buildings were opened in the Strand in 1882. Even the King's Bench, over which in theory the monarch himself presided, ceased after Richard II's time to follow him on tour, and came to rest at Westminster.

Until late in John's reign most of the legal work was in the hands of the clergy. One of the oddest things for a modern mind to grasp is that most of what we call 'professional' people were at this period at least nominally in holy orders, though for practical purposes they were occupied as civil servants or civil engineers, biographers or military architects. The situation was now changing, nowhere more abruptly than in the legal sphere. In 1207 it was

Beginnings of a bureaucracy: the Court of Exchequer (*left*) and the Court of Chancery.

45

decreed that the clergy should not plead in secular courts. Thenceforth the lawyer was a layman. A new close-knit professional community sprang into existence and set its lasting mark upon the face of London.

The Inns of Court belong to the next reign. Edward I was much concerned with the functioning of justice, and he was fortunate in his principal adviser, Henry de Lacy, Earl of Lincoln, who saw the importance of a proper scheme of education for intending lawyers. Edward set up two royal commissions on the legal system, and it was after the second, in 1292, that Lincoln's Inn was founded. This and the subsequent Inns of Court were intended, like the halls and colleges springing up for scholars in Oxford and Cambridge, to serve as residential hostels for the men of law. But they also had an educational function. Young men studied the law and divinity. They also learned dancing, singing and some musical instrument, for the intention was to equip them not only for the 'court' in a legal sense but also for the other 'court' in which social accomplishments would help their advancement. In the next few centuries the Inns of Court, besides creating the legal profession, provided London with the equivalent of the university it did not possess, for many country gentlemen and others, who had no thought of becoming lawyers, entered one or other of the Inns to acquire general polish, a useful smattering of law, and social connections. By Elizabeth's time, when Oxford and Cambridge were in the doldrums, the Inns of Court were especially popular. Walter Ralegh, for example, after a brief spell at Oxford and sundry other adventures, is found in the Temple, though in later years he strenuously denied that he had ever studied law. And it was in Middle Temple hall, by tradition, that *Twelfth Night* had its first performance in 1601. Certainly the masques and revels of the various Inns had by that time become famous.

In Edward's time the emphasis was more strictly legal. Lincoln's Inn was followed by others, though precise dates are hard to fix. It seems that loose communities of lawyers grew up in a particular locality and only after many years became formally constituted as an Inn. Thus the Temple, which became two, the Inner Temple and the Middle Temple, can point to no reliable documentation before 1449, but the buildings were leased to certain professors of the common law as early as 1338. The old round church became the accepted rendezvous of lawyers and prospective clients, as did the sheltered porch of St Paul's and the precincts of Westminster Hall.

Gray's Inn, on a site owned by Lord Grey de Wilton, was in existence before 1370. Besides these four Inns of Court there were the numerous Inns of Chancery, such as Staple Inn (the façade of whose later Elizabethan building survives), Clifford's, Clement's, and others that are now mere names on modern walls. These gave a simpler legal training, suitable for the Chancery clerks, but men could proceed from them to the Inns of Court. The Chancery itself found a permanent home in the lane that still bears its name. It was established on the site of the present Public Record Office, just after Simon de Montfort's defeat and death at Evesham in 1265. There must have been a good deal of reorganization at that time. Henry III had been travelling round the country as Simon's hostage, sulkily endorsing the policies of the rebel earl. He was to live another seven years but already it was his energetic son, the Lord Edward, who was pulling together the distracted kingdom he was to inherit.

Edward had fought Simon to the death, but he was too intelligent not to take over what was valuable in his innovations. Simon had sown the seed of the future House of Commons. Edward let it grow. Parliaments still met briefly, at long intervals, and with limited functions. But from this time forward, apart from abnormal occasions such as Charles II's calling of a Parliament at Oxford as late as 1681, Westminster was the recognized venue. Soon the Commons began to hold their meetings separately from the Lords. They used whatever accommodation was available, sometimes the Painted Chamber, sometimes the Chapter House, sometimes the Refectory. In 1547, after the Reformation, they were to take over St Stephen's Chapel, and adapt it as best they could as a debating chamber. It served them until the fire of 1834, and was the setting for most of the great scenes in Parliamentary history, Charles I's furious intrusion, Cromwell's 'bauble' outburst, and the rhetorical displays of Burke.

Thus, by the fourteenth century, the royal household, the day-to-day public administration, the proceedings of the law courts, and the meetings of Parliament, however occasional, were all firmly based on London, making that city in every sense the nation's capital. There were obvious social consequences.

Even in Saxon times many a bishop and nobleman had seen the convenience of possessing his own town house in London. Now every man of rank found it essential. These town houses became more magnificent and more continuously occupied. The favourite sites were along the north bank of the river, on the slope below the Strand, though that important highway between London and Westminster did not acquire stone paving until Richard II's reign. North of the Strand stretched the 'convent garden' belonging to the Westminster monks. On the south the line of mansions stretched from the Temple along the waterfront until it reached the Royal Mews, then located where Trafalgar Square is now.

Conspicuous in this line rose the Palace of the Savoy, built in 1246 for Peter of Savoy, the uncle of Henry's Provençal queen. Henry's gift of this spacious site was a good example of that generosity to his foreign in-laws which made him so unpopular with Englishmen. In the following century the palace was held by the Duke of Lancaster, John of Gaunt, and among the many notable men who regularly crossed its threshold were his protégé, Chaucer, and his unwitting political instrument, Wycliffe.

Bishops were thick along the Strand. Carlisle and Chester, Exeter and Worcester, Llandaff and Durham, were all near neighbours in those early days. When the golden age of the medieval prelates was over, and the new men of the Tudor era took their place, these laymen did so literally along the Strand – we find Walter Ralegh, for example, installed in Durham House. The bishops never, of course, had a monopoly of the area. Besides the Savoy, there were other mansions occupied by the nobility. One was Hungerford House, built for Lord Hungerford, where Charing Cross Station stands today. The name survives only in the useful foot-bridge that carries concert-goers to the Royal Festival Hall across the river. Few of them could give the origin of that name, but many would confidently and incorrectly explain 'Charing' as derived from Edward I's '*chère reine*' whose funeral progress the Cross certainly did commemorate. The 'Charing' is older, however, probably the Old English *cierring* or 'turning', an allusion either to the sharp bend of the Thames at this point or to a similar bend in the old Roman road running westwards.

There was not space along the Strand for every bishop. Fulham Palace, further up the river, had been the home of London's own bishops since 1141, and Canterbury was established at Lambeth, where Archbishop Langton had begun the building of a palace in King John's reign. The crypt dates from about 1200 and the little chapel, which has seen the consecration of so many bishops, from about thirty years later. Soon after that, the Archbishop of York made his London home at York Place, later Whitehall.

The Bishop of Ely made his London base in Holborn, where his house provided the setting for John of Gaunt's famous death-scene in *Richard II*. The Duke did in fact die there, having lost his own Savoy Palace eighteen years earlier, burnt down by Wat Tyler's men. In another play, *Richard III*, Shakespeare puts these words into the mouth of the future king:

> My Lord of Ely, when I was last in Holborn
> I saw good strawberries in your garden there;
> I do beseech you, send for some of them.

The Bishop returns with the fruit only thirteen lines later, which, since the request is made in 'A Room in the Tower', seems express delivery indeed. When, in Elizabethan times, a later bishop was coerced into leasing this renowned garden to Sir Christopher Hatton, he managed to reserve the perpetual right to walk in it and to gather twenty bushels of roses every year. Today

Edward I, while famous as a warrior, did much too to make London a centre for orderly litigation.

this spot is Hatton Garden, centre of the diamond trade. The sole relic of the Bishop's house is its beautiful little Gothic chapel, built in 1290, but Ely Place is still a private precinct with its own beadle. By a legal oddity it retained, right down to modern times, a kind of extra-territorial status, ranking as a scrap of Cambridgeshire in London.

There was another kind of development in thirteenth-century London, which is similarly traceable in place-names. Henry's reign saw the first arrival in England of the friars, and Henry, for all his preoccupation with his beloved Benedictine abbey at Westminster, was extremely generous to the new mendicant fraternities. The dark-habited Dominicans made their first settlement in Holborn: then, after half a century, early in Edward's reign, they moved down to the neighbourhood of the two obsolete fortresses, Baynard's Castle and Montfichet, the area known ever since as Blackfriars. The Franciscans, or Grey Friars, started in Cornhill but in 1224 built their friary further west in Newgate Street. The Carmelites reached London in 1241: Edward later gave them a site between Fleet Street and the river, where Whitefriars Street and Carmelite Street still record their presence.

Other friaries were established during the thirteenth century. The Crutched, or 'Crossed', Friars had their home near the Tower. Near Broad Street the Austin Friars occupied a big site, with their own church and churchyard, cloister and gardens, an illustration of the demands made on the limited space of the city by these multiplying communities. Yet another order, the Friars of the Sac, began outside Aldersgate and moved to Old Jewry in 1290.

That was the year Edward expelled the Jews from England. There had been an influx of Jews in the wake of the Normans. London had had a considerable ghetto since the Conqueror's time, and for more than two hundred years the Jews had made their constructive contribution to the life of the city, despite the usual sad sequence of persecution and prejudice, occasionally flaring up into a pogrom. After Edward's intolerant edict there were no more Jews in London, or indeed in England, except during a brief period under Elizabeth, until Oliver Cromwell removed the ban. Few of the Elizabethan playgoers who hooted Shylock could ever have seen a member of his race. The immediate consequence of the exodus in 1290 was that money-lending and other financial operations passed to the control of Italians, as yet another famous place-name, Lombard Street, reminds us. The native Londoners had yet to acquire the flair and finesse that were to be the City's boast in later times.

The monastic life. *Above,* a nun playing a psaltery. *Below,* adultery leads to the stocks, and the laity, unencumbered by vows of chastity, point the finger of scorn.

Jewish moneylender's office. Barred from many occupations by their inability to take a Christian oath, the Jews were at least free from the Church's prejudice against usury. So, before their expulsion in 1290, they played a key role in commerce and banking, despite the occasional flare-up of violence (*left*).

Life in the Plantagenet capital offered much the same mixture of splendour and squalor – and not infrequent savagery – as could have been found in any of the other great European cities of the period. The mere list of exalted visitors to Henry III's court, all welcomed with appropriate display, gives some hint of the pageantry to which the working Londoner was treated from time to time. There were embassies from the Holy Roman Emperor and from every corner of Christendom, from Scotland and Norway, Portugal and Bohemia.

Envoys arrived even from the Sultan of Damascus and from that pictur-esque but sinister potentate, the Old Man of the Mountain, ruler of the Assassins. His representative came in the summer of 1238. Nine years later,

Westminster had to welcome no less a guest than the Emperor of Constantinople in person, the impecunious Baldwin II. On that occasion Henry was put to considerable charges, for, apart from the cost of the festivities, he had to give his visitor '500 marks of the best money' and a further thirty marks, or twenty pounds, for his expenses. The latter sum was not, of course, expected to go far along the homeward road to Byzantium. The Constable of Dover Castle had instructions to pay Baldwin's passage across the Channel, at which point England's responsibility presumably ceased.

Most if not all of these colourful visitors must have passed across Peter de Colechurch's new stone bridge, which provided not only a suitably impressive approach to London but a ready-made grandstand for the townsfolk to enjoy the spectacle. And it was the setting for much more elaborate processions, such as the welcome in 1236 to Henry and the bride he had just taken in Canterbury, an occasion which incidentally offered a convenient excuse for a fresh coronation ceremony in Westminster Abbey. Henry's original crowning, as a child, had taken place at Gloucester, London then being in the hands of his late father's rebellious barons.

Another great day for London Bridge was 2 August 1274, the homecoming of Edward I from his crusade. It was the city's first sight of him for four years, in the middle of which his father's death had made him king. Such occasions as that the Londoner could hardly expect to see more than once or twice in a lifetime. In October 1347 there was Edward III's triumphant return from the French war. In 1357 there was the Black Prince, home from Poitiers with the captured King of France and a string of other illustrious prisoners. That scene, it was said, was never matched until the similar return of Henry V from Agincourt, over half a century later. On that day the mayor and aldermen went out to meet him at Blackheath in their scarlet gowns, with four hundred other citizens clad in mulberry, and escorted him to the bridge, all brilliantly decorated, with the royal arms displayed on banners from its towers. And the welcome at London Bridge, needless to say, was only the opening of festivities that continued through the streets from end to end of a delirious city.

Behind this splendour lay the squalor and the poverty. The squalor was, to a certain extent, shared by all classes. The stench of the Fleet river, for instance, so appalled the Carmelite friars that they complained to the King. The mayor and aldermen did what they could to improve things. They made regulations, they punished offenders, they provided such elementary public services as the medieval mind could conceive, and they made some effort, however tardy and ineffective, to remedy grievances. Each ward had a public privy. The Ludgate privy was continually criticized for its neglected condition. 'It makith an orrible stench and foul sight,' says one record. It had often been reported but 'no remedye yit is ordeined'. Twelve carts carried refuse out of the city to dumps in the suburbs, and boats were used to collect it from the areas bordering the river. Butchers' offal and similar waste constituted a special problem. Here the scavenging was done by the birds. A Bohemian visitor to London wrote that never in his life had he seen so many kites. They strutted and flapped about the narrow streets unmolested. Indeed, it was an offence to harm them. The function they performed was far too valuable.

Opposite Edward III in the robes of the Order of the Garter.

Roy : r : dward :

Mass burial of Black Death victims at Tournai, Belgium, in 1349. The death-rate in London may well have been over ten thousand – more than a third of the capital's population.

The poverty that existed, side by side with the opulence, may be gauged from the list of Henry III's charities. The sheriffs were instructed, in 1245, to buy three hundred pairs of shoes for distribution to the poor at Christmas: we know even the prices, fourpence-halfpenny, fivepence or fivepence-halfpenny a pair. On another occasion there was ten pounds to feed the poor in the King's great hall at Westminster, 'as many as can get in'. Such items recur again and again. Henry, with all his faults and extravagances, was a kindly man, and it would be unfair to dismiss the payments as conscience money to offset his lavish expenditure in other directions. He cared for individuals, and the accounts are full of small payments, gifts in kind, and thoughtful provision of services to persons in need. But this generosity went, inevitably, to cases he knew about – to his childhood nurse, to one of his wife's maids who lost her sight, to one of his clerks for some family emergency – and one wonders what happened to all the other hard cases that had no connection with the royal household. There were, of course, the other rich and noble households, there was the charity dispensed by the friars and other churchmen, and there was the rudimentary welfare service operated by the guilds for their own members, widows and orphans. Even so, plenty of empty bellies must have been left. The phrase, 'as many as can get in', is eloquent. If there was such a throng at Westminster Hall on that particular day, where did they eat for the rest of the year?

It was a hundred years later, in November 1348, that the Black Death struck London, sweeping up from the south-west where it had first arrived from the stricken Continent. There are no statistics for the city as a whole, only grim indications such as the death-roll at Westminster Abbey, where the abbot himself and twenty-six of the monks succumbed. When, in 1371, one of Edward III's commanders, Sir Walter de Manny, endowed a new Carthusian monastery, the famous Charterhouse, it is still said that he built it on a site 'where 50,000 victims of the Black Death had been interred'. As the total London population was well below this figure, which was never reached before about 1530, it prompts the question, 'Where did they come from, and who buried them?' But the mortality may have been well over ten thousand, for it is usually reckoned that England lost one-third of her people, and it would be remarkable if the proportion was not higher in the crowded capital. There were two lesser outbreaks in 1361 and 1368, but it seems unlikely that the Charterhouse site would have been used for the burial of these additional victims – or that, if so, Sir Walter would have built on the ground so soon afterwards.

Plagues were a recurrent feature of London life for the next three centuries. Though it is the first and the last, the Black Death and the Plague of 1665, that are best remembered, there were sixteen major outbreaks in between, some of them lasting for several years. Who now speaks of the epidemic in 1603, the year of James I's accession? Yet it killed 38,000 Londoners, and when his son came to the throne in 1625 another outbreak killed nearly as many. By that date there were Bills of Mortality, so that there is an official figure, 35,417, which can be accepted as roughly accurate. So both these outbreaks cost well over half the lives lost in the final terrible catastrophe of 1665, when the mortality rose to 68,596. This was out of a population then approaching half a million. One in seven is bad enough. If the Black Death in 1348 took one in three, its impact on London may be imagined.

Against the scale of these calamities the violence of man to man seems almost insignificant, but it was an element in London history that cannot be ignored.

Henry III and his family knew the horror of a hostile mob. The citizens favoured Simon de Montfort against him. The foreign Queen and her relatives were especially unpopular. On one occasion, when the royal couple were staying in the Tower, none too happy with the background murmur that reached their ears from outside, Henry decided to send Eleanor to the greater safety of Windsor. As road-travel was unthinkable, she started up the Thames in the royal barge. But London Bridge so swarmed with a threatening multitude, prepared to shoot and shower missiles down upon her, that she was forced to turn back.

Failing an outside enemy or an alien community such as the Jews within their midst, the ebullient townsmen were quite ready to fight each other. Guild jealousy was a common cause. Thus in 1267, as soon as peace had returned to the kingdom after the Barons' War, London saw a bloody street-battle between the goldsmiths and the tailors, in which the cloth-workers and cordwainers were soon involved. Five hundred men joined in the affray, a number were killed and wounded, and thirteen ringleaders were hanged.

Guild rivalry also played its part in the seizure of the city in the so-called Peasants' Revolt of 1381. But that was such a dramatic episode in London's history that it deserves a chapter to itself.

5

Wat Tyler and Walworth

Wat Tyler's death at Smithfield, with Mayor Walworth striking the fatal blow and the boy King spurring forward towards the rebel host with the shouted pledge, '*I* will be your leader!', is one of the great set-pieces of English history. Less familiar is the sequence of events which placed London, normally able to defy even a disciplined army, at the mercy of the peasants. And William Walworth, apart from his brief hour of dubious glory, remains to most people otherwise unknown. The whole background, however, is worth study for what it reveals of London life at the time.

Walworth came as a youth from Durham, like many who found their way to the capital at that time to fill the labour shortage caused by the Black Death. He was apprenticed to John Lovekyn of the Fishmongers' Guild. Clearly he prospered and, for an outsider, established himself remarkably well in the city. He became an alderman in 1368, succeeding to the place of his former master. He was sheriff in 1370, mayor for the first time in 1374. He moved to a large mansion in Thames Street on the site where the Fish-mongers' Hall, one building or another, has stood since soon after his death: in the present hall is preserved the dagger with which he is said to have stabbed Wat Tyler. Apart from that one act, he was clearly a man with due regard for the processes of the law, for in his will he left his brother an unusually fine collection of legal books.

In the course of his business Walworth leased the 'stews' or fish-ponds in Southwark from the Bishop of Winchester, whose town house stood near by. The fishmonger had also an interest in the other, quite different 'stews' in the same neighbourhood, the riverside brothels which owed their shorter name to the ambiguous reputation of the public bath-houses in those days.

Stow recalls that these latter 'stews' had existed in Southwark 'time out of mind' until they were suppressed by, of all monarchs, Henry VIII. There were at one period eighteen houses, with signs painted on the walls facing the Thames, identifying them like inns as the Bell, the Swan, the Cross Keys, and – somewhat irreverently – the Cardinal's Hat. They were subject to strict regulations. The women were not to be exploited or intimidated by the stew-holder. Patrons were not to be importuned or given short measure. 'No single woman to take money to lie with any man,' it had been solemnly enacted at Westminster right back in Henry II's reign, 'but she lie with him all night till the morrow.'

Walworth owned these houses and leased them out to a Flemish promoter. They were only one of his subsidiary interests. The chief fishmongers were very big businessmen, wholesalers, whose trading connections stretched far

Opposite Meeting of Wat Tyler and John Ball before the march on London. Ball, an excommunicated priest, preached at Blackheath to the rebels on the theme 'When Adam delved and Eve span, who was then the gentleman?'

Funeral pall (*c.* 1500) used at the lying-in-state of members of the Fishmongers' Company. Attractive mermaids provide a recurrent motif.

out beyond the city boundaries, and as Edward III's long reign drew to a close Walworth was a dominant figure in London. To quote Stow again: 'these fishmongers having been jolly citizens, and six mayors of their company in the space of twenty-four years', the Durham lad had won his way to the forefront of an oligarchy which aroused great envy in other quarters and produced the disunity so perilous to the city when the Wat Tyler crisis came.

Throughout the whole of the fourteenth century London had seen those stirrings of class struggle – the conflict between the 'big' men and the 'little' men – that can be traced in the history of the Italian trading cities at this time. In London the basic issue was whether the government should be run by a small self-perpetuating clique, the mayor, sheriffs and aldermen chosen from the major guilds, or whether there should be a common council elected on a ward system, evolved from the rudimentary democratic procedure of Anglo-Saxon days, giving more say to the humbler townsmen. The details, and the vicissitudes of the struggle, decade by decade, would require a specialist and scholarly volume, but it needs only a little imagination, and acquaintance with the politics of our own century, to sense the atmosphere. Walworth looms through the mist as a familiar figure. His opponents can be confidently pictured before they are even mentioned. The uproar and the arguments, recurrent in most communities and in most centuries, contain few surprises.

Walworth's principal opponent was John of Northampton, a draper. The grouping of the guilds was determined by their economic interests. The Fishmongers were allied with the equally powerful Grocers and the other 'victualling' trades. Against them stood the Drapers, Mercers, Taylors, Goldsmiths, Saddlers, Haberdashers, and in general the 'non-victuallers', who resented the stranglehold of the monopolies enjoyed by their enemies, especially the monopoly in fish, so indispensable to a Catholic diet. The city masses naturally wanted cheap food. The non-victualling trades identified themselves with the masses, not so much from philanthropy as from the knowledge that low prices would enable them to pay their journeymen low wages.

In 1376, the year before Edward III's death, there was a storm over the proposal to shift power from the wards to the guilds. The old King bestirred himself and threatened to intervene. Walworth went with a deputation to reassure him. Edward was persuaded that there had been no disorder, only a warm debate, which we can almost hear Walworth describing as a 'frank and useful exchange of views'.

Early in 1377 the conflict grew warmer, though oddly cloaked by a quite different pretext. John of Northampton was a friend of John of Gaunt, who for his own reasons was supporting Wycliffe against the Bishop of London's charge of heresy. Wycliffe came to answer the charge at St Paul's. Gaunt escorted him. Northampton, a sheriff that year, escorted them both with a band of followers. This provoked the Fishmongers and their allies. They attacked the procession and in the riot Gaunt had to run for his life, and his Palace of the Savoy nearly met, that day, the fate that befell it four years later.

Edward died. As Duke of Lancaster and uncle to the child King, Gaunt was virtual ruler of the country. He took his revenge on the hostile London victuallers by calling the 1378 Parliament not to Westminster but to Gloucester, with a consequent loss of profit to Walworth and his fellow-traders.

They too were not lacking in ingenuity. The disorder of the previous year – above all, the tongue-in-the-cheek dismay at the attack on the noble Duke – had provided a pretext to depose the mayor, Adam Staple, a mercer, and replace him with a grocer, Nicholas Brembar. The victuallers were then firmly back in the civic saddle. Two more grocers followed. In 1380 it seemed time for their fishmonger allies to take a turn, and Walworth began his second spell of office, stretching into the fateful year of 1381.

Great Seal of Edward III, with the orb in his left hand. The old king's last days were troubled with conflict between the city's rival guilds.

This was the background of London politics, therefore, when the imposition of a fresh and heavier poll-tax, the third in four years, roused the whole of south-east England to revolt.

The first news of serious trouble reached the city late on Sunday 2 June, when Sir Robert Belknap, the chief justice of the Common Pleas, arrived in a state of shock. He had been down to Brentwood to inquire into a local riot against the tax-collectors, and had found himself beset by an armed mob. His escort of pikemen had been overwhelmed, his papers had been burned, he had been made to kneel and swear that he would never come down on such a mission again. Three of his clerks and three tax-assessors had been lynched. At that moment their heads, mounted on poles, were being paraded round the Essex villages.

Across the estuary, Kent simultaneously flared into revolt. During the next day or two, terrified fugitives streamed into London with stories of looted manor-houses, bonfires of parchment rolls, and occasional murders of unpopular local figures or hapless aliens like the Flemish merchants in Colchester. For a little while Walworth may have seen the trouble as an affair of the countryside, the 'Peasants' Revolt' it is still called, something not likely to concern him officially as mayor of London. Within a week he knew better. On Tuesday 11 June, a host of Kentish rebels headed by Wat Tyler and John Ball set out from Canterbury to march on the capital. Simultaneously the Essex men advanced on Aldgate.

The defence of London devolved on the mayor. The fourteen-year-old King Richard had been at Windsor but had come to the Tower for greater safety. There, in Henry III's great concentric fortress, within the moat and curtain walls that Edward I had added, and with a garrison of six hundred men-at-arms and six hundred archers, the boy should be out of reach of the rebels. His mother, the Fair Maid of Kent, now joined him there. She had been on pilgrimage in Kent and had run the gauntlet of Wat Tyler's men. She brought her own alarming stories of a countryside aflame.

The crisis could hardly have come at a worse moment. Apart from the Tower garrison there were almost no troops within call: they were far away on the Welsh and Scottish borders or beyond the Channel. The King's three uncles were equally unavailable. John of Gaunt, the strongest and also the most unpopular man in the kingdom, was on a peace mission in Edinburgh. It was perhaps as well for him: the rebel demands included his head and those of the chancellor, treasurer, and every prominent member of the government, fifteen in all. Walworth, however bitterly opposed he was to Gaunt, may have wished wholeheartedly for his presence just then. Gaunt had at least seen military service, though he had never shone as a commander. As it was, there was a vacuum which the fishmonger, as mayor of London, must do his best to fill.

By the Wednesday evening, 12 June, the Kentish rebels were encamped on Blackheath, having covered the march from Canterbury at a speed few generals would have attempted. Walworth made sure that London Bridge was closed against them. But another horde from Essex had reached Mile End. Walworth had the gates shut, but would mere gates and walls keep out such a desperate multitude if there was no adequate garrison to defend them? Here

John of Gaunt, brother to Edward III and uncle of the boy King, Richard II. He took sides in the guild rivalries and was a highly controversial figure in London.

Opposite King Richard II in his youth. Detail from the Wilton Diptych.

the disunity of the Londoners coincided fatally with the paralysis afflicting the Court. It was either impossible or too dangerous to muster the citizens under arms. In their divided ranks there was far too much sympathy for the rebels, far too much hatred of the King's present advisers, far too much inter-guild mistrust.

That night, from his house in Thames Street, Walworth may have heard the uproar from just across the river, where a forward part of the Kentish men had pushed right on into Southwark and joined with the local dissidents. He may have seen the sky redden with fire and even known the cause: one of his bawdy-houses was in flames. Frustrated by the raised drawbridge, the rebels broke open the two prisons on the south bank, the Marshalsea and the King's Bench, and let out the inmates. One party pushed on to Lambeth Palace, hoping to catch Archbishop Sudbury, whom they had missed at Canterbury and whom they had sworn to kill. Sudbury was unpopular because of his political role as chancellor. He had taken refuge in the Tower, along with the treasurer, Sir Robert Hales, and other councillors on the rebels' black list. That night the mob could only sack Lambeth Palace and burn the parchment rolls.

The next morning the King took the royal barge down to Greenwich and, in another famous scene, tried to negotiate with the Blackheath rebels crowding the banks. They had nothing against the boy personally. Throughout the rising they protested their loyalty to the Crown, while demanding a clean sweep of his advisers – and by decapitation, not merely dismissal – and the concession of radical reforms. Discussion under such conditions was impossible and it would have been clearly unwise to let the King step ashore and become a hostage. Walworth must have been thankful when the barge returned safely to the Tower, and not surprised that the trip had been abortive.

Only one thing was on the side of the authorities: time. Though the rebels appeared to possess leaders of surprising ability and decision, they could not keep their huge makeshift armies together for long. Hunger alone would disperse them if they could not get at the food stocks within the city. But, in his determination to keep them out, Walworth had not sufficiently allowed for divergences among his own followers.

It was another fishmonger, Alderman John Horne, who failed him. With two other aldermen Horne had been sent across the river the previous evening to talk to the rebels and dissuade them from acts of violence. Horne had held a private conversation with Wat Tyler and been won over. Returning, he had reported reassuringly to the mayor. He had not mentioned that secretly he had brought back with him three of the rebels, who were now spreading their propaganda through the city.

Now, on the morrow, after that fruitless confrontation at Greenwich, Tyler's host flooded into Southwark and packed the end of the bridge until the gap at their feet brought them to a halt. What happened next is uncertain. One story is that Horne recrossed the river, presumably by boat, with a royal standard which he had obtained by a trick. Moving to the head of the column and waving this, he induced the alderman in charge of the gate to let down the drawbridge. Both aldermen were afterwards accused of treacherously admitting the rebels to the city, but both were eventually acquitted. It may be that they were overwhelmed by a mob of townsmen who sympathized with the revolt. As matters stood in London that year, acquittal by a jury proves nothing.

Anyhow, the bridge – which had defied so many earlier attackers – was yielded to Wat Tyler's men without a blow. Almost at the same time, another alderman belonging to one of the rival guilds threw Aldgate open to the rebels from Essex. Chaucer was at this time living in the house over the gate, but, though a prominent public servant and a protégé of John of Gaunt, he seems not to have been involved in the wild scenes that followed. From two directions the rebels streamed into the city and merged with a mob of genuine sympathizers and unscrupulous opportunists.

This time the Savoy was not spared. John of Gaunt's superb palace was burnt out, the damage increased by the ill-advised action of those who threw three barrels of gunpowder on to the flames. A looter was seized and tossed into the fire. Tyler had ordered that there should be no looting. Priceless hangings and robes, silver plate and coin, all were to be destroyed not stolen.

Geoffrey Chaucer in his last days, living in straitened circumstances in Westminster.

The Fleet Prison was invaded, the captives let out. Parties broke into the Temple, burning records and murdering lawyers. Flemings and Italians were hunted down and killed, even the seven wretches who had taken sanctuary in the church of St John's Priory at Clerkenwell, where the adjoining hospital smouldered for a week afterwards. Houses were burnt in Holborn and Fleet Street. Cheapside ran with blood.

Amid this chaos there was not much that Walworth could do. His own preference for decisive action was overruled by the Earl of Salisbury, who, like most professional soldiers, had a healthy distrust of being drawn into street-fighting against a hostile population. Walworth wanted to gather such forces as they had, the Tower garrison and a small draft of soldiers that Sir Robert Knollys had been mustering for Brittany, and make a surprise attack during the night which might drive the rebels into panic-stricken retreat. The Earl would not accept such a gamble. Appeasement was in the air. The King's immediate idea was to distract the rebels and draw them away from the Tower, so that Sudbury, Hales and the other individuals most threatened should have a chance to slip to safety.

Richard sent Walworth his orders. He was to pass them on to the sheriffs and aldermen, to proclaim in their wards that 'on pain of life and limb all between the ages of fifteen and sixty should be at Mile End on the morrow, Friday, and meet him there at seven of the clock.' Walworth saw it was done, and himself joined the small royal party that rode out to meet the concourse of rebels at Mile End outside the walls. It was a tense hour. There were thousands of rebels, but by no means all of them. Wat Tyler seems not to have been there. One party, under Jack Straw, was out at Highbury, burning the treasurer's new manor-house. Another was attacking the house of the under-sheriff of Middlesex at Westminster. And a good number were still watching the Tower lest their victims escape. Archbishop Sudbury tried, but he was recognized as his boat put out from the water gate, and he had to go back.

Richard made promises to the crowd at Mile End and a number drifted away satisfied. But his main objective, to save the lives of his councillors, was not achieved. How the mob broke into the Tower remains unexplained.

The murder of Archbishop Sudbury at the Tower. Sudbury's political role, as Chancellor, won him the hatred of the masses.

Obviously the garrison put up no resistance. Just as, the day before, the rebels had stormed across London Bridge, now they took possession of the citadel which once the Conqueror and Rufus had planned to dominate the population, and which later kings had made impregnable to normal attack. Sudbury, Hales and several other unfortunates – including a friar whose only crime was to be John of Gaunt's physician – were dragged out of the chapel and executed on Tower Hill. The Archbishop's head, complete with mitre, was carried round the streets before being set up on the gates of London Bridge. John of Gaunt's son, Henry Bolingbroke, the same age as his cousin Richard whom he was later to depose, was saved by a loyal servant. Richard's mother fainted in the middle of that nightmare scene, and her pages carried her off to the Queen's Wardrobe, formerly known as the Tower Royal, in the Vintry Ward some distance away. There Richard found her, and stayed the night. After the horrors of the day hope was at its nadir.

The next day was Saturday. Richard had only one idea, to keep talking with the rebels, to communicate, and if possible to negotiate. It is hard to see what else he could have done. He told Walworth to call another mass meeting, this time at Smithfield, and to announce that he wished to hear the rebel demands. The gathering was summoned for five o'clock in the afternoon. It was a hot day, near to midsummer.

Walworth and his own small party waited for the King at St Bartholomew's Church. Across the open space was the great mass of the rebels, armed and 'terrible with banners'. This time the King's escort numbered two hundred riders, but they looked nothing against the horde confronting them. They had put on armour under their long robes and so had Walworth, wisely as it proved.

There are various accounts of the dialogue that followed between Wat Tyler and the King, and of the scuffle that ensued. One version is that Walworth, unable to bear Tyler's insolence any longer, pulled him off his horse; another that Tyler tried to stab Walworth in the stomach but was foiled by the hidden armour of the mayor, who drew his own weapon and cut the rebel leader across the neck, after which a squire named Standish struck the finishing blow. However it started, there is no doubt that Tyler was killed and that after a very ugly minute or two, when the entire royal party could easily have been overwhelmed and torn to pieces, the magnetism of the young King held the crowd and calmed them.

Walworth, ever the realist, slipped quickly from the scene – not to save his skin, but to do what he had been longing to do, to muster Sir Robert Knollys's mercenaries and any resolute, dependable citizens he could get hold of. He was back with them at Smithfield while the King was still talking. Now the tables were turned. Leaderless and hesitant, the rebels, for all their numbers, could have been driven into panic-stricken rout and massacred. But Richard, in that brief contact with the commons, had sensed how many of these men were honest and innocent of violence, pressed into the revolt by intimidation and false assurances. He would have no massacre. The rebels dispersed quietly.

Walworth's service met with immediate reward. Then and there, Richard insisted on knighting him. Stow says that the fishmonger protested that 'he

was neither worthy nor able to take such estate upon him, for he was but a merchant, and had to live by his merchandise only.' Notwithstanding, the boy took a sword in both hands and 'strongly stroke him on the neck, as the manner was then'. Sir William did not enjoy his honour for many years. He died in 1385.

Wat Tyler, about to draw his sword against the King, is struck down by Mayor Walworth. This is a composite picture, in which King Richard figures twice: on the right, he is winning over the rebels after the death of Wat Tyler.

6

'The Flower of Cities All'

There is a radiant word-picture of late medieval London by William Dunbar, who came south in 1501 to promote the marriage between King James IV of Scotland and Henry VII's small daughter, Margaret Tudor. Dunbar was as skilful a courtier and diplomat as he was a poet. Whatever honeyed words he murmured in Westminster, he did not fail to grasp the importance of the London merchant class. To them primarily he directed his poem, 'In Honour of the City of London', each verse concluding with the refrain:

> *London, thou art the flower of cities all.*

Through the Scot's appreciative eyes we can see the renowned river,

> *Where many a swan doth swim with winges fair,*

and the ships at anchor and the barges plying up and down, some rowed, some under sail. In a few lines Dunbar sketches in the bridge 'of pillars white', the 'merchants full royal to behold', and the 'seemly knights' passing along the streets

> *In velvet gownes and in chains of gold.*

He speaks of the 'blithe' churches and the sound of all their bells – this is still a Catholic London, full of monasteries and friaries – but quickly he returns to the splendours of the bourgeoisie:

> *. . . Rich be thy merchants in substance that excells;*
> *Fair be their wives, right lovesome, white and small;*
> *Clear be thy virgins, lusty under kells:*
> *London, thou art the flower of cities all.*

The 'kells' or cauls were a net-like headdress of decorative thread.

It was not surprising that the London ladies made an impression upon the poet. Erasmus, visiting England about the same time, commented on the number of 'married women and damsels' who were actively engaged in commerce and industry, and there is plenty of documentary evidence for it. But it was something else that especially appealed to the Dutch scholar and to many other visiting strangers:

To mention but a single attraction, the English girls are divinely pretty, soft, pleasant, gentle and charming. . . . They have one custom which cannot be too much admired. They kiss you when you arrive. They kiss you when you go away and they kiss you when you return. Go where you will, it is all kisses, and, my dear Faustus, if you had once tasted how soft and fragrant those lips are, you would wish to spend your life here.

Opposite The Tower of London, about 1500, with London Bridge in the background.

'City of spires' – the earliest printed view of London, printed in 1497 by Wynkyn de Worde.

Earlier, in 1466, a Bohemian described how 'at the first arrival of guests in any lodging, the hostess with all her household comes forth into the street to receive them; and each one of them it behoves each one to kiss. Indeed to them to take a kiss is, as to others, to offer the right hand; for they are not used to offer the hand.' The custom continued a long time. Nicander Nucius, a Greek visitor to London in 1545, excused this female forwardness: 'To themselves this appears by no means indecent.' They were still at it in the days of Bunyan, who tactlessly inquired why, if the kissing was no more than a polite convention, 'did they salute the most handsome, and let the ill-favoured go?' Despite the Puritans, the casual kissing did not stop until the eighteenth century, when increasing sophistication brought more formal manners. César de Saussure, visiting London from Lausanne in 1725, still observed that many women were offended if not thus warmly greeted, but that 'some of the ladies who have travelled in foreign countries now offer their cheeks instead of their lips.' Erasmus would have seen this, sadly, as the beginning of the end.

Dunbar does not mention the kissing itself. Having paid graceful but general tribute to the ladies, he concentrates his eulogy on the men, who would have more direct influence on the negotiations. The smugness and insularity of the English were already bywords with other nations. Only four years earlier, Andrea Trevisan, the Venetian ambassador to London, had reported after attending a four-hour banquet given by the mayor to a thousand guests: 'The English are great lovers of themselves and of everything belonging to them. They think there are no other men than themselves and no other world but England.'

So Dunbar, with a proper sense of climax, devotes his closing stanza to civic dignity:

> Thy famous Mayor, by princely governance,
>   With sword of justice thee ruleth prudently.
> No lord of Paris, Venice, or Florence
>   In dignity or honour goeth to him nigh.
>   He is exemplar, lode-star, and guy;
> Principal patron and rose original,
>   Above all mayors as master most worthy:
> London, thou art the flower of cities all.

Needless to say, 'guy' is used in its contemporary meaning of 'guide'.

Poetic flourishes allowed for, Dunbar's picture is not much exaggerated. The wealth of London in the late Middle Ages was formidable indeed. Even the sardonic Venetian had to admit it. Visiting Goldsmiths' Row in Cheapside he counted fifty-two goldsmiths' shops. 'In all the shops in Milan, Rome, Venice and Florence,' he reported, 'I do not think there would be found so many of the magnificence that are to be found in London.' Dunbar's glorification of the mayor as the apex of this social pyramid is justified by the facts.

The mayors of this period were often outstanding personalities. The roll of their names epitomizes a good deal of the city's history. Walworth was not the only man of action. Sir John Philpot, a grocer, 'sent ships to the sea, and scoured it of pirates,' Stow records, 'taking many of them prisoners.' He became mayor the following year, 1378. Richard II's reign was an eventful period for the civic heads. Walworth's rival and successor, the reforming mayor, John of Northampton, offended many of the vested interests and was 'committed to perpetual prison' in Tintagel Castle, from which remote and romantic stronghold he was delivered only by the influence of his friend, John of Gaunt. Another controversial figure was Sir Nicholas Brembar, a grocer, champion of the victualling guilds and a dependable royal supporter. He was executed, with many of Richard's other adherents, when the King's victorious enemies assembled in the 'Merciless Parliament' of 1388.

Four years later, when Richard was furious with the city for refusing him a thousand-pound loan, he suspended its civic liberties and removed the hapless mayor, a draper named John Hend, to imprisonment in Windsor Castle. He himself flung off to Nottingham for the whole summer, taking not only his Court but the Chancery department. A deputation of twenty-four burgesses, including Henry Yevele, the renowned architect of Westminster Hall, had to travel to that midland town and persuade him to return. He did so grudgingly, and the city that had refused him a loan was forced into

Westminster Hall, rebuilt at the end of the fourteenth century by Henry Yevele, has the biggest timber roof constructed in the Middle Ages. Hammer-beams, a yard thick and seven yards long, end in flying angels. Hugh Herland was the carpenter who produced this oaken masterpiece.

providing an obsequious and expensive welcome home, with presentations of golden crowns and wine-cups.

From those early days of turmoil provoked by Wat Tyler, Richard's relationship with the Londoners seems to have been constantly shadowed with dissension and suspicion. He had occasion to summon a parliament in 1397 when the great hall at Westminster was under repair. It is noteworthy that, instead of being able to use this as an excuse to meet some distance from London, he had to provide a temporary structure of timber, with a tiled roof, in the palace courtyard. Stow tells us that it was 'very large and long . . . open on both the sides and at both the ends, that all men might see and hear what was both said and done.' The security problem must have compared with the worst of modern conditions, for Stow goes on to describe how 'thousands' of the royal archers, Cheshire men, 'compassed the house about with their bows bent, and arrows notched in their hands, always ready to shoot; they had bouch of court (to wit, meat and drink), and great wages of six pence by the day.' Alas for Richard! When Yevele finished his restoration of the permanent hall, and parliament resumed their meetings there, one of the first scenes enacted in 1399, under the magnificent oak roof we see today, was the King's own deposition. His abdication document was signed in the Tower.

Richard's extravagance antagonized the merchant princes of London. They were more willing to accept the financial demands of warrior kings such as Edward III and Henry V, for, under the veneer of chivalry, those victories at Crecy and Agincourt had a down-to-earth relevance to economic interests abroad. Edward IV, again, though a free spender, learned to pay for his own amusement and not nag the citizens for grants and loans.

To call these leading citizens 'merchant princes' is no exaggeration. They had now long since passed the stage of being merely the foremost London tradesmen in their own line of business. They had mostly ceased to be retailers at all, and their commercial tentacles reached out far beyond the city. In the clothing trade, for example, the big London merchants controlled the clothworkers in the country areas, gave credit to small-town dealers and wandering chapmen, and formed partnerships with the landowners who went over, increasingly, to wool production. Overseas, they had their links with Bruges and Florence and other great trading centres. Learning from the shrewd Italians and Flemings, they were soon familiar with the more sophisticated commercial techniques, the manipulation of credit, the convenient involvement of sleeping partners, and the art of speculating in futures.

There is a picturesque anecdote, quite credible if not impeccably documented, about that most famous merchant prince of all, the mercer Dick Whittington. When Henry V brought home his beautiful French bride, Whittington gave them a banquet regardless of expense. Even the huge log fire was given extra fragrance by casting on handfuls of costly spices. The Queen remarked upon the cost. Whittington said he would make it even more expensive, and promptly threw into the flames a handful of bills for a total of £60,000 owed him by the King. As a public-relations exercise, combined with the realistic writing-off of bad debts, the gesture certainly makes sense.

Whether or not this incident happened, the known facts of Whittington's life are worth summarizing, for in many ways he was typical of the merchant princes Dunbar described.

To begin with, he was not a native Londoner. Secondly, he was from the gentry, the third son of a Gloucestershire knight. These facts illustrate the geographical and social fluidity of the period. A large proportion of these leading citizens had roots in the provinces: if they did not retire there, they often remembered their birthplace by endowing local schools and alms-houses. Conversely, many a Londoner who prospered in trade went on to buy land and establish a county family. If such families made the complete transition from commerce to country gentry, they were balanced by the gentlemen's younger sons who, like Dick Whittington, went to London to seek their fortune and were not despised for it.

Whittington prospered as a mercer. He was made an alderman in 1393, when he was in his early thirties, and became sheriff soon afterwards. Four years later the mayor, Adam Bamme, died in office. The King appointed Whittington to take over the office until the October election, when the city confirmed him in it for the ensuing year. He served again in Henry IV's reign in 1406 and in 1419 under Henry V. Whether he is regarded as serving three times or four depends on the separate reckoning of that initial term. Clearly he was *persona grata* with all three monarchs. He supplied the trousseau for Henry IV's daughter Blanche at her wedding to the Duke of Bavaria and for her younger sister Philippa when she married the King of Denmark in 1405.

Like his fellow merchants, Whittington lived in a fine mansion comparable with any of the town houses or 'inns' occupied by noblemen and bishops. It stood between Cannon Street and Thames Street, near St Michael Paternoster Royal, the church in which he was buried. The site of the house is

The wealth and position of a Mayor of London are symbolized by Richard Whittington's death-bed. Priest, monk and physician, servants and friends watch the passing of a distinguished man.

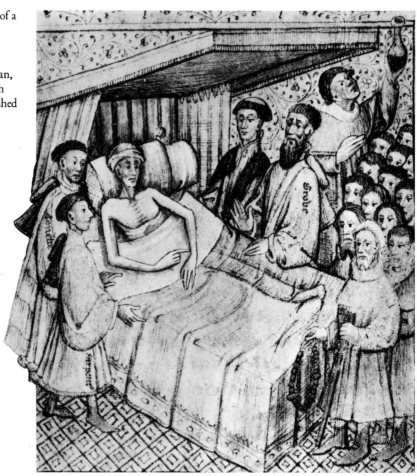

still known as College Hill, from the collegiate institution and almshouses he founded there. In his generous charities Whittington was also typical, though perhaps even more generous than most, since, though he did actually marry Alice Fitzwarren, as in the story, they died childless and, for that matter, catless – there is no historical basis for the cat – and the Whittington wealth could be lavished exclusively on good causes.

These included the rebuilding of Newgate Prison, whose foul conditions had appalled him, and of St Bartholomew's Hospital. He also made substantial contributions to Guildhall, which was established by the combined efforts of the various guilds as a centre for the government of the city. A mere cottage was, in the years following 1411, replaced by an impressive block of buildings. Whittington's money paid for a floor of Purbeck marble and glass windows embellished with his arms. It also met half the cost of the library, with its twenty-eight desks, its settles and its wainscoting, together with the services of a librarian.

Whittington was one of several fifteenth-century benefactors who provided conduits for pure water. Other mayors concentrated on the repairs of highways, walls and gates. Some acted swiftly in emergencies: in 1390 the goldsmith Adam Bamme 'provided from beyond the seas corn in great abundance, so that the city was able to serve the country', and in 1438, when 'wheat sold for three shillings the bushel', the grocer Stephen Brown 'sent into Prussia, and caused to be brought from thence certain ships laden with rye, which did great relief'. Leadenhall was originally built as a common granary by the draper Simon Eyre, and only later became a famous market. Eyre left endowments for a Leadenhall chapel and a school, with alternative charitable uses for the money if these were not established, as in fact they were not. 'Neither', says Stow darkly, 'how the stock of three thousand marks, or rather five thousand marks, was employed by his executors, could I ever learn.'

Simon Eyre, draper and Mayor in 1445. It was he who built Leadenhall (*top*). This view of the City (*c.* 1540) shows the present Leadenhall Street, crossed by Gracechurch Street (to the south) and Bishopsgate Street. The winding lane is Lime Street, with St Mary Axe opposite.

73

Some, like the sheriff Philip Malpas, concentrated on the material comfort of the unfortunate, providing 'every year for five years 403 shirts and smocks, forty pairs of sheets, and 150 gowns of frieze to the poor'. Others used their term of office to promote an improvement in morals. In 1472 Sir William Hampton, a fishmonger, 'punished strumpets, and caused stocks to be set in every ward to punish vagabonds'. A later mayor, in 1503, the draper Sir William Capell, substituted a cage for this purpose. Yet idleness and wickedness persisted.

In Whittington's time the mayors were almost entirely chosen from the principal guilds, 'the Great Twelve' as they were called. There were dozens of others, some very rich and 'minor' only in official status. These included the brewers, whose ostentatious banquets (especially the swans) made their rivals jealous. In 1377, when Whittington was probably an apprentice, London had just over fifty guilds. By the turn of the century there were more than a hundred. When he died in 1423 the list of crafts and trades ran to 111, but there were frequent amalgamations, hatters with haberdashers, spurriers with blacksmiths, fullers and shearmen with clothworkers. Whittington's mercers, though not the oldest association, acquired precedence among the city companies. Edward III was not too proud to accept honorary membership and was the first royal freeman claimed by any of them. Each was headed by a Master, sometimes called the Prime Warden, assisted by several wardens and a clerk, with a chaplain and a beadle. Former masters and wardens served on the Court of Assistants, a kind of governing body working with the officers of the year. Each guild acquired in time its own hall, often the town house of some nobleman. Nearly all the original halls were burnt down in 1666 and those that were rebuilt suffered almost as severely in the 1940 blitz. Then, out of the thirtyfive halls, seventeen were destroyed and another fifteen badly damaged.

At Guildhall the mayor and the two sheriffs presided over the city very much as they would have run the affairs of their own guild, though on a larger scale. The title 'Lord' Mayor crept in by degrees. It was not regularly used until 1545, though the mayor already enjoyed equal precedence with viscounts and mitred abbots. Knighthood – exceptional at first, as in Walworth's case, and never conferred on Whittington – became a customary honour in 1519, and ten years later it was laid down that no man should serve twice in the office. Gradually the mayor acquired an impressive entourage, while in 1471 the sheriffs 'were appointed each of them to have sixteen sergeants, every sergeant to have his yeoman, and six clerks; to wit, a secondary, a clerk of the papers, and four other clerks, besides the under sheriffs' clerks, their stewards, butlers, porters, and other in household many.' The bureaucracy of local government was not invented yesterday.

In 1383 it was laid down that no one should be mayor until he had acquired experience as a sheriff, but this was not invariably observed. By Elizabethan times Stow could point out that many a mayor had never been sheriff, but had been advanced straight from alderman. 'A grave and learned lawyer' served as recorder, and took precedence in court and council before all but former mayors. Ever since King John's time a new mayor had been required to go to Westminster, take the oath and receive royal approval. This was the genesis

of the Lord Mayor's Show. In 1453 a draper named John Norman was the first to make the ceremonial journey by river. In 1501 Sir John Shaa, a goldsmith, combined both forms of spectacle by having all the aldermen escort him on horseback to the point of embarkation in his barge. It was this mayor who first held his banquet at Guildhall, building on kitchens for the purpose.

Probably it was a close relative of his, Edmund Shaa, another goldsmith and mayor in the summer of 1483, who at that crucial moment backed the Protector, Richard, in his successful claim to the crown. Edmund's brother, Dr Shaa, preached at Paul's Cross, a favourite place for such propagandist manifestos, arguing against the legitimacy of the 'princes in the Tower', as they are now remembered. But our second mayor Shaa was either on the other side or had joined it two years later, for it was Henry VII who dubbed him 'Sir John' on the field of Bosworth.

Throughout the Wars of the Roses, the dynastic conflict at last resolved on that day in Leicestershire, the merchant princes in general favoured the Yorkists. They had little enthusiasm for the last of the Lancastrians: Henry VI, doomed to the throne from infancy, grew up to demonstrate all too clearly that he was neither Henry IV nor Henry V. A meek, pious, prudishly modest sovereign, he crept diffidently round Westminster Abbey seeking space for his future tomb, and would stop the boys from his newly founded college at Eton to warn them against the moral perils of his own Court at near-by Windsor. Education was Henry's passion. Besides founding Eton and King's College at Cambridge, he obliged the Mercers, in the charter he

The Lord Mayor's Show, in one form or another, dates back at least five hundred years. The Livery Companies vied with each other in lavish contributions. This was the Fishmongers' in 1616.

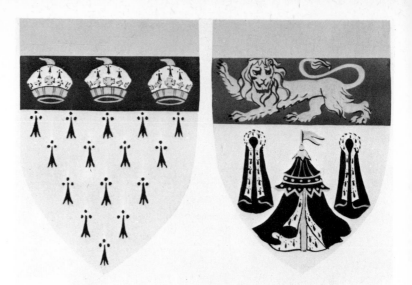

Arms of the Skinners' Company (*left*) and the Merchant Taylors.

granted them in 1444, to found a grammar school which did London good service for the next five centuries. But, while the merchants had nothing against education within reason – at different dates the Merchant Taylors, the Haberdashers, the Brewers, the Grocers, the Skinners and others all endowed schools either in London or elsewhere, at Tonbridge or Oundle or Aldenham – they had interests closer to their hearts and pockets. They were ready for a stronger government than Henry's, once it was offered.

Jack Cade's rebellion in 1450 was a kind of prelude, no more than a demonstration, but for a few grim days it brought back memories of Wat Tyler. Events followed a similar pattern, with an army of Kentish rebels encamped at Blackheath, the occupation of Southwark, and the lowering of the drawbridge by London sympathizers. For five days Cade boasted himself lord of the city. As before, there were demands for reform and the dismissal of unpopular ministers. As before, several unfortunate scapegoats were beheaded. But Cade preferred to keep his headquarters south of the river, sleeping each night at the White Hart in Southwark, and on the seventh morning he saw the drawbridge raised against him. He tried to force the crossing, only to find, like so many earlier attackers, that London Bridge was impregnable if properly defended. So Cade's rebellion fizzled out, and a week later its wounded leader died miserably in a cart bearing him to prison. Whatever London's impulsive sympathy with the popular discontent, the realistic merchants preferred to wait for a genuine alternative government.

Their chance came in 1461. Edward of York, having avenged his father's death by a victory at Mortimer's Cross, marched south and was welcomed by enthusiastic crowds at Clerkenwell. A Yorkist-dominated council declared him King and he was duly proclaimed Edward IV. Another victorious battle, at Towton, clinched the matter and sent the hapless Henry into exile. Edward established himself firmly in London, and took special care to cultivate the merchants. A complete contrast to Henry – a handsome giant of a man, dashing, hail-fellow-well-met – he was congenial in both personality and policies. He became quite literally one of them, for he entered into business on his own account, exporting wool and cloth on a large scale and at a handsome profit. This increased his popularity by making him less dependent on taxes and loans, ever a bone of contention between the merchants and their monarch. They loved a commercially minded king who could even partially pay his own way. His luxuries and scandals were willingly forgiven. He dined in their houses; he invited not only the mayor and aldermen but even lesser citizens to join his hunting parties in Waltham Forest. That he occasionally shared not only their business interests but their wives, notably Jane Shore, was a minor drawback which distressed only those personally affected.

Who could deny that Edward IV was the right king – or at least the right king for London? So, when Henry was induced to attempt a counter-revolution, few questioned the decision, when he was captured, to clap him into the Tower, as soft in the head and unfit to rule.

Henry remained in the Tower from 1465 to his mysteriously convenient death in 1471, except for the few months when a Lancastrian coup sent Edward briefly into exile in Flanders. With Henry's captivity and probable murder begins the most sombre period of the Tower's history. Before that, like any other fortress, it had held its share of famous prisoners, kings of Scotland and France and the poet Charles, Duke of Orleans. Some, such as the patriot William Wallace, had met their end there. But it was particularly in the few decades starting from 1471 that the Tower won its reputation as the scene of murderous liquidations within the royal family and those with any possible claim to the crown. Henry VI, then Edward IV's brother George, the Duke of Clarence, then Edward's two sons, and finally anyone, whether Clarence's son or Perkin Warbeck, who could conceivably threaten Henry Tudor, were successively eliminated within its walls.

The Londoners themselves, even the most eminent, can be acquitted of complicity in these murky affairs, which for that relatively short period merely reproduced in their city what in Italy would have passed as unremarkable. The announcement of Henry VI's death must be recalled in its context. So much happened in a few weeks. Edward landed in Yorkshire in March to win back his throne, was warmly welcomed back to London on 11 April, and taking Henry as his prisoner marched out again to defeat Warwick the Kingmaker at Barnet three days later. Then, when all seemed over – Warwick dead, Henry safe back in the Tower in custody, Edward's triumphant followers disbanding – news came that Henry's more bellicose queen had returned from France and was raising an army in the south-west. Edward got his men together again and marched across to defeat that second army at Tewkesbury on 14 May, and it was in that very week, while he was far from his capital – to which he might very likely never return alive – that London was attacked by another force of his enemies. This was led by a follower of the dead Kingmaker Warwick, the picturesquely named 'Bastard Fauconberg'. London Bridge held firm against him, though Stow says that he 'burnt the gate, and all the houses to the drawbridge, that time thirteen in number'. More persistent and resourceful than some, Fauconberg tried to land on the north bank from boats, but the whole waterfront from Baynard's Castle down to the Tower was stoutly defended. Finally, crossing the river

outside the city limits, he made attempts on various gates, culminating in an assault on Aldgate where a storming party managed to get inside. This party was then isolated from the main body by the lowering of the portcullis, and wiped out, after which the defenders raised the portcullis again, made a sortie, and finally routed the attackers.

After a month or two of these excitements the ordinary Londoners can scarcely be blamed if they heard the news of Henry VI's death in the Tower on 24 May without being unduly moved. Now, perhaps, they reflected as they crossed themselves, the country might enjoy peace.

And so, until Edward's death in 1483, it did. Foreign trade expanded rapidly, and the Londoners increased their domination at the expense of the provincials. In Southampton, for instance, they first took over much of that port's oversea business and then transferred it to London. Two national organizations that had started in Edward III's reign, the Company of the Staple dealing in wool and the Merchant Adventurers dealing in everything else, but especially cloth, were largely controlled by their London members, who monopolized the offices and raised entry fees to discourage applicants from outside. Only in one field did the London businessmen have to acknow-ledge defeat: even Edward's favour could not help them against the German cities of the Hanseatic League.

For centuries the merchants of the League had been firmly entrenched in the heart of London, occupying the Steelyard upstream from the bridge, where Cannon Street station was later to be built, and living their own insular life with extra-territorial rights. The Londoners, always apt to hate aliens, whether Lombards or Flemings, especially resented the privileges of the Hanse. There was a common saying, 'The Hanseatic merchant buys a fox-skin from an Englishman for a penny, so that he can sell him the tail for a florin.' The Germans refused to admit Englishmen to membership, and the Company of Merchant Adventurers was formed, largely by the mercers, to compensate for this exclusion. Edward tried to close down the Steelyard, but the League retaliated with a crippling embargo on English cloth abroad. In 1473 Edward gave in. Hanseatic privileges were restored, compensation paid, and the Steelyard site, hitherto on lease, granted as a freehold. The League held firm to all its rights even under the formidable Henry VII. Its monopoly survived effectively until the middle of the sixteenth century and its legal position was not finally abolished until the last years of Elizabeth. The actual site remained the property of the League, itself a kind of historical ghost surviving the Thirty Years War, and was only in 1852 sold to an unromantic Victorian railway company.

One new trade London owed to Edward. During the months he spent as a fugitive in Flanders, he met Caxton. Caxton had been out of England for thirty years. His apprenticeship to a silk mercer had been broken by his master's death and he had left London for Bruges to complete his training. He had been prominent in the Merchant Adventurers when they had their overseas headquarters there, and about this time he became commercial adviser to Edward's brother-in-law, the Duke of Burgundy. He did not become a printer until a few years later, but then it was not long before, in the autumn of 1476, he had set up his press under Edward's patronage in

Opposite Edward IV – 'the right king for London'. He took care to cultivate the businessmen.

Westminster, where he soon attracted many customers from among the merchants as well as the nobility. He had always thought of himself as a Londoner, though born in Kent and so long resident abroad. One of his own translations, *Caton*, was dedicated: 'unto the noble, ancient and renowned City, the City of London in England, I, William Caxton, citizen of the same, owe of right my service and good will. . . .' His assistant, Wynkyn de Worde, moved subsequently to Fleet Street and then again to St Paul's churchyard, and henceforth it was in these two areas that London's printing and publishing developed.

Richard III, if he had lived, would not have neglected the London merchants, even though his style might have been less convivial than his brother's. In his brief time as Protector, before taking the crown himself, he made his headquarters at Crosby Place in Bishopsgate. This house had been built in 1466, 'of stone and timber, very large and beautiful, and the highest at that time in London', for Sir John Crosby, a grocer and former sheriff. Some idea of the magnificence of those late Plantagenet town houses may be gained from its hall, which escaped the fire that destroyed the rest of the mansion in the seventeenth century and was skilfully removed and re-erected in

'The Squire', by Wynkyn de Worde, from the Caxton *Canterbury Tales*. A native of Alsace, de Worde was the first to establish publishing in Fleet Street and St Paul's churchyard.

Opposite: Recuyell of the Historyes of Troye, translated from the French by Caxton, was the first publication from his own press. The translator-printer is presenting a copy to Edward IV's sister, Margaret of Burgundy, at Bruges. A year or two later he transferred his printing to Westminster.

Chelsea in 1910. It is easy to understand why, in Elizabethan times, the house was judged worthy to accommodate various foreign embassies. In that summer of 1483, when Richard was mobilizing political support for his take-over, it was an ideal base from which to operate.

Two years later, all that was old history, and the aldermen were adjusting themselves to a new sovereign. Henry VII has been well described as 'incomparably the best business man to sit upon the English throne'. Though he began in debt and at once borrowed another three thousand marks from the Londoners, he repaid the loan so promptly that they were always ready to lend again. Soon, by rigorous economy and financial flair, it was he who was the lender. Continuing the general policy Edward had begun, he negotiated an advantageous commercial treaty with the Netherlands. More and more trade flowed between Antwerp and London. It was the booming London of the first Tudor that Dunbar visited and eulogized.

Henry did not stint on building. He added rooms to the Palace of Westminster and completely restored Baynard's Castle. On the ruins of the Savoy he built the hospital of St John the Baptist to take a hundred poor inmates. When the palace at Shene was burnt, he rebuilt and renamed it Richmond Palace. But his favourite residence on the outskirts of London became Duke Humfrey's Palace of Placentia, which he refaced with bricks, a building material disused after Roman times, reintroduced from the Low Countries

Timber roof of the Great Hall, Crosby Place – taken down and re-erected in Chelsea, it is all that remains of a great town house of Plantagenet times.

Opposite Richard III. He used Crosby Place, then in Bishopsgate, as his headquarters before he seized the crown.

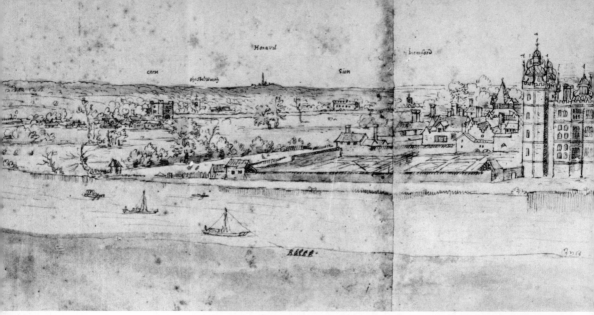

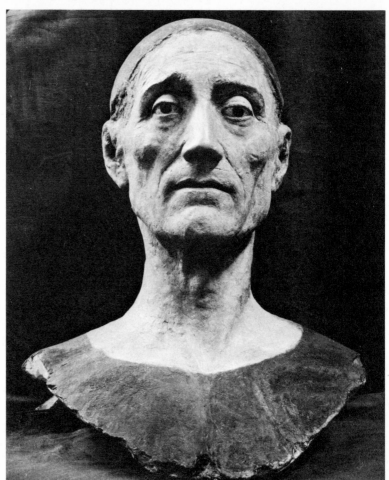

Above Richmond Palace: drawing by Antony Wyngaerde. Only a gateway survives of the splendid Tudor palace in which Elizabeth died.

Right Henry VII, 'the best business man to sit upon the English throne'.

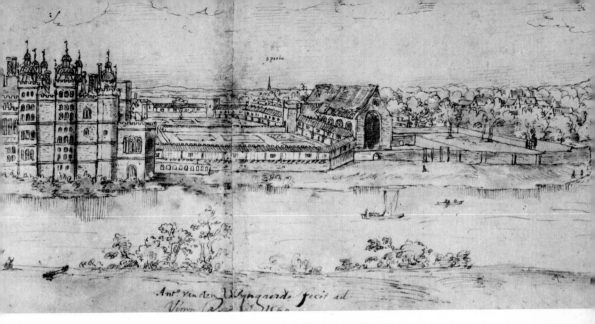

Ant° van den Wyngaerde fecit ad
Vinum [...] 1544

under the name of 'Flanders tiles', and not widely employed before the fifteenth century. This palace he rechristened Greenwich. It saw the birth of Henry VIII, Mary and Elizabeth, who regularly spent her summers there, though she died at Richmond. Another palace at Kensington, dating from the Black Prince's time, was abandoned by Henry VII.

Early in his son's reign, in 1512, most of the Palace of Westminster was badly damaged by fire, and it was never completely restored. Henry VIII's jealous eyes were roving elsewhere. Wolsey was just beginning to build his lavish mansion at Hampton Court and, being newly made Archbishop of York, to extend and embellish York Place, his official London house adjoin-ing Westminster. When Henry broke Wolsey, he seized both palaces, renaming the second one 'Whitehall'. Not content with these, he began in 1531 the construction of St James's Palace on the site of an ancient leper hospital, and in 1538 he commissioned Nonsuch, that fantastic italinate creation in Surrey so regrettably passed on by Charles II to Lady Castle-maine and demolished by her as a profitable essay in property development.

Something else, with much more important consequences, was taking place while Henry was adding to his palaces. This was the decade of the Reformation Parliament and the dissolution of the monasteries, making the real end of medieval England and, more specifically, changing the face of London, where hitherto the various religious houses had occupied so much of the city area itself and owned so much of the land outside, blocking expansion in the suburbs.

The Dissolution, though a shock when it came, was not of course an historical accident, provoked by the personal problems of a king. The monasteries had long been under severe criticism within the Church. 'What, my lord,' cried the Bishop of Exeter in 1514, 'shall we build houses and provide livelihood for a company of bussing monks, whose end and fall we may live to see?' Even the zealous Cardinal Pole advised the Pope that most of the Orders should be disbanded and a fresh beginning made. If this was the view of eminent churchmen, the attitude of the average London layman is not hard to guess. The enterprising merchant class had developed a new ethic which, better or worse, was in conflict with the more static medieval Catholic view of the world. London was already predominantly anti-clerical in the early years of Henry VIII, long before he laid a finger on the monasteries. Ideology and the self-interest of the new capitalists were in convenient harmony.

So, when the moment came, and in default of any coherent scheme for the take-over of monastic properties, there was a rather ungodly scramble for bargains. The pattern traceable in countless small towns and villages over England was reproduced every few hundred paces in the crowded city. Some of the convents and friaries were adapted into private mansions, others were demolished for the value of their building materials and their sites. The poet, Sir Thomas Wyatt, built himself a fine house where the Crutched Friars had been and swept away their church to make his tennis court. The Charterhouse passed through various hands. Sir Edward North, the lawyer, raised a mansion where the cloisters had stood: here subsequently Elizabeth stayed several days before making her official entry into the city at the time of her accession, and James was welcomed before his coronation. Finally, in 1611, the property was bought by Thomas Sutton, a wealthy coal-owner and versatile venturer, who established the still-existing charity from which the famous public school evolved.

Some conventional churches were taken over to serve parishes, but at least one, at St Martin-le-Grand, was destroyed to make way for a tavern. Even where buildings were retained, their precincts and gardens were often filled in with shops and dwellings. Whitefriars, by a legal anomaly, retained its ancient right of sanctuary even though the Carmelites were dispossessed: for another century and a half, until 1697, the rabbit-warren of tenements and alleys that spread over the site served as a kind of nature reserve for evil-doers of every type, and acquired the name 'Alsatia' from the disputed No-Man's-Land between France and Germany, since no magistrate or constable had jurisdiction there. Greyfriars became – under Edward VI, in whose brief reign so much of the aftermath of the Dissolution had to be dealt with – the nucleus of another famous public school, Christ's Hospital. Blackfriars was granted to Henry VIII's first Master of the Revels, Sir Thomas Carwarden, who stored costumes there and probably held rehearsals: later it served as a theatre, first for the child actors and eventually for Burbage's company.

South of the river, the monastery dedicated to Becket's memory was bought by the citizens and continued as St Thomas's Hospital for 'poor, sick and helpless objects'. It remained in Southwark until 1871 when it moved to Lambeth.

Westminster was more fortunate. The recently completed Henry VII's Chapel would alone have guaranteed the protection of his son. The monastery, of course, went. The dispersal of so important an establishment was a blow to the neighbourhood, for while the monarch was only occasionally in residence in the adjoining palace the monks had been always there, providing trade and employment. Henry designated the abbey church as one of his new cathedrals, but in fact there was to be only one Bishop of Westminster. Mary

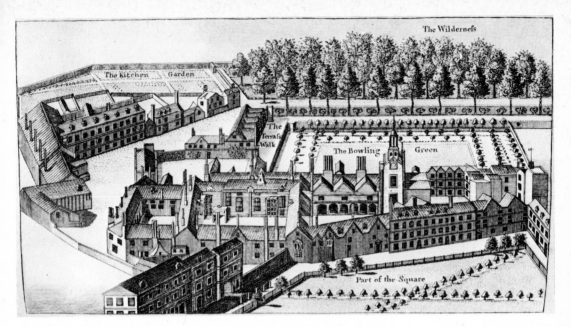

The Wildernefs

The Kitchen Garden

The Terrafs Walk

The Bowling Green

Part of the Square

tried to restore the monastery. Her sister reversed that, but gave the church its present status as a 'Crown peculiar', with its dean and chapter subordinate only to the sovereign. Many of the other buildings also survive. The abbot's house is now the deanery, the monks' dormitory is the muniment room, and their refectory is the dining-hall of Westminster School.

Even where developers had a free hand and acted with indecent speed, the replacement of monastic London could not be carried out overnight. Even in 1553 a foreign ambassador at Mary's Court was writing sadly of the scene that had so delighted Dunbar half a century earlier: 'The city is much disfigured by the ruins of a multitude of churches and monasteries belonging heretofore to friars and nuns.'

Formerly a monastery of the Carthusian monks, the Charterhouse (in what is now Charterhouse Square) was bought in 1611 by Thomas Sutton. Here he set up a school for forty poor boys, which developed into the well-known public school subsequently transferred to Godalming.

7

'Storehouse and Mart of All Europe'

London's population had grown slowly during the Middle Ages and had taken a long time to pass that of Roman London at its height. Under the Tudors the rate of growth quickened. Trade and industry expanded. The dissolution of the monasteries, while creating space for development in the city, caused unemployment in other parts of England, for, while the monks and nuns were offered pensions, there were no redundancy payments for the countless laymen to whom they had given work, not only as monastery servants but in the various productive enterprises connected with this religious order or that.

Parallel with this, or often actually coinciding with it, was the effect of the change from arable farming to sheep, occasioned by that very expansion of the export trade in woollen cloth which was central to London's prosperity. It meant anything but prosperity for the rural workers whose labour was no longer needed. Many of these too flocked to London, sometimes in such hordes that the authorities were seized with panic and had to take emergency action. The boy King, Edward VI, was roused to sympathy by one of Ridley's sermons on the subject: he wrote to the Lord Mayor, a committee was formed, and the establishment of St Thomas's Hospital and other charities followed, but these provided only for the helpless, and the rest, the 'sturdy beggars', had to find work and shelter as best they could, or face the deterrent consequences. Later in the century came yet another influx, when religious persecution on the Continent caused large numbers of Flemings and Huguenot Frenchmen to seek refuge under a Protestant queen.

Opposite Georg Gisze, a Hanseatic merchant at the London Steelyard, *c.* 1532: portrait by Hans Holbein the Younger. The English merchant venturers had a long, hard battle against these powerful foreign competitors with their entrenched privileges.

Sturdy beggars and 'vagabones', though discouraged by a whipping at the cart's tail, presented a permanent problem to the civic authorities in Tudor London.

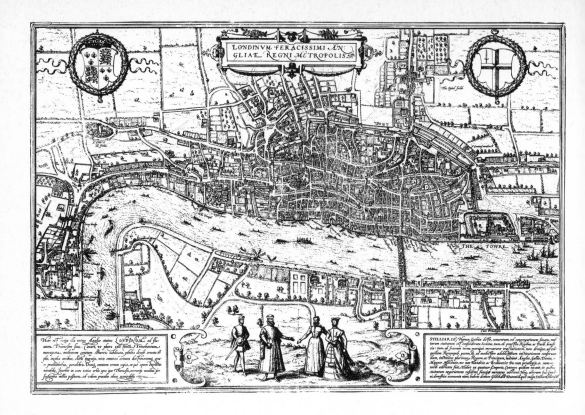

Map of London by Braun and Hohenburg, 1572. The thickly populated area stretches from the Tower in the east, north as far as Smithfield, to Somerset House in the west, but scattered buildings are shown as far up-river as Lambeth Palace.

When Henry VIII came to the throne in 1509, the population of London was about 50,000, only 10,000 more than it had been in the reign of Richard Lionheart. It had put on another 12,000 before the Dissolution of the Monasteries. Thirty years later, in 1563, according to the estimates of modern scholars, it had leapt to over 90,000. By 1583 it was 120,000. At Elizabeth's death in 1603 it must have been about 200,000, having more than doubled itself during her reign and more than tripled itself since the closure of the monasteries.

That closure provided only part of the space needed to house the vast increase. Within its old boundaries the city was built up as never before. The houses rose higher, the upper stories were thrust out over the lower. Most streets were little more than canyons. There were only a few of any width. One was Cheapside, where the ancient Cross set up by Edward I for his dead Queen served as a natural gathering-place for the reading of proclamations, and the conduit, bringing pure water in lead pipes from Paddington, was the rendezvous for household servants and the professional water-carriers who delivered it in tall wooden vessels, hooped with osier, to any home that would pay for the service. Cheapside, running on eastwards into the Poultry and Cornhill, was the axis on which the city's life revolved. Another wide thoroughfare lay to the north, what is now known as London Wall. It followed the inner line of the fortifications and had escaped being built on for obvious military reasons. Apart from these streets and a few others the Londoners had to shoulder their way through narrow lanes, and it is not

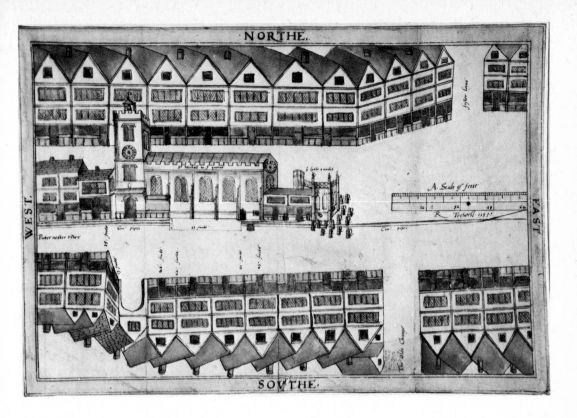

Ralph Treswell's careful plan of Cheapside and Paternoster Row (1585) shows one of the conduits bringing drinking water from the Tyburn. The tall wooden cans, hooped with osier, stand ready. The church is St Michael-le-Quern, never rebuilt after the Great Fire.

surprising that, where possible, they turned with relief to the plentiful water-men plying for hire up and down the river.

And London itself was spreading up and down that river. Sir Thomas More settled at Chelsea, where his guest, Erasmus, described his 'modest yet commodious mansion' – it needed to be 'commodious' to hold his four married children, their spouses, and his eleven grandchildren. But this gracious sort of residential development was as nothing compared with the changes below London Bridge. Henry's naval enthusiasm caused him to establish royal dockyards at Deptford and Woolwich, and all along the north bank opposite spread the rash of building that was so much to distress John Stow when, in late Elizabethan times, he looked back on the rural beauty he had known in boyhood.

Born about 1525, son and grandson of respectable London tallow-chandlers, Stow began as a tailor but never went far in the trade. The past was his passion – fortunately for us, for without his tireless seeking out of old manuscripts and records we should know much less of London up to 1598, when his *Survey* first came out. 'He was tall of stature,' wrote his friend Edmond Howes, 'lean of body and face, his eyes small and crystalline, of a pleasant and cheerful countenance; his sight and memory very good; very sober, mild, and courteous. . . . He always protested never to have written anything either for malice, fear, or favour, nor to seek his own particular gain or vain-glory; and that his only pains and care was to write *truth*.' Stow was perhaps the first author to express that intense nostalgia which characterizes so much of the

The alabaster tomb of John Stow in St Andrew Undershaft. The pen is annually renewed in April, in grateful memory of his work on London's history.

best English literature. He recalls lovingly the unspoilt environs of London in his childhood, when he would be sent from his home on Cornhill to fetch a halfpennyworth of milk from Goodman's Farm the other side of Aldgate, and all round the city lay open fields. But in seventy years much had altered, and nowhere more than down-river from the Tower.

Here, wrote Stow, was 'a continual street, or filthy strait passage, with alleys of small tenements, or cottages . . . inhabited by sailors' victuallers.' In his youth, 'not to be forgotten', the first buildings at Ratcliff had been a free school and almshouses, 'but of late years shipwrights, and (for the most part) other marine men, have built many large and strong houses for themselves, and smaller for sailors, from thence almost to Poplar, and so to Blackwall.' It was the same elsewhere. East of Aldgate, both sides of the road were 'pestered with cottages and alleys, even up to Whitechapel church, and almost half a mile beyond it, into the common field; all which ought to be open and free for all men . . . this common field, I say, being sometime the beauty of this city.'

Further from the Thames, development came more slowly. St Giles's and St Martin's remained literally 'in the fields' for some time longer, and where Leicester Square is now was still 'Lammas land', thrown open to pasture in August after the hay or corn had been cut. The name 'Soho' traditionally derives from a hunting-cry and for another century that area was parkland. North of the city, settlement was discouraged by the clay which there lay on the surface, at once rendering drainage difficult and preventing the collection of drinking water in deep wells.

Moorfields, the marsh where Fitzstephen had long ago loved to watch the skaters, had a varied history which Stow tells us in some detail. Early in Henry V's reign the mayor had begun to drain it and build causeways so that people could walk across to Islington and Hoxton, but about sixty years later another mayor, wishing to repair the city wall, had clay-pits dug for brick-making, 'by which means this field was made the worse for a long time'. In 1512 another effort was made. Ditches were dug, 'with bridges arched over them' for walkers, but the improvement was partial and still the field 'stood full of noisome waters' and 'overgrown with flags, sedges, and rushes'. The final and effective drainage scheme was begun in 1527, when the mayor 'caused divers sluices to be made to convey the said waters . . . into the course of the Walbrook, and so into the Thames; and by these degrees

Laundresses at work in Moorfields in about 1560 – after it had been drained, and footpaths laid out.

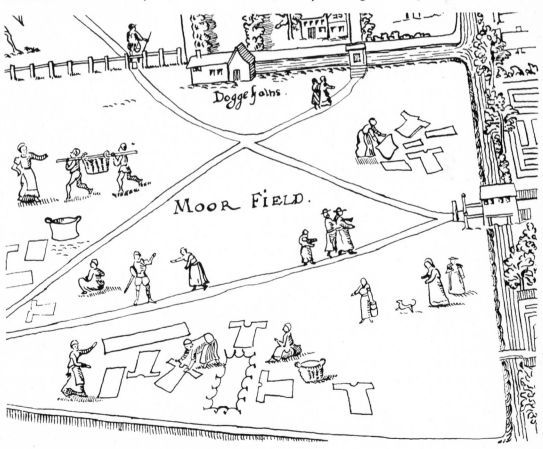

was this fen or moor at length made main and hard ground.' With its foot-paths and little bridges it became more than ever a popular place of resort.

The Londoners were jealous of these open spaces and opposed any attempt to enclose them. Edward Hall, an earlier chronicler, recounts the story of a violent demonstration early in Henry VIII's reign. 'Before this time,' writes Hall,

the inhabitants of . . . Islington, Hoxton, Shoreditch, and others, had so enclosed the common fields with hedges and ditches, that neither the young men of the city might shoot, nor the ancient persons walk for their pleasures . . . either their bows and arrows were taken away or broken, or the honest persons arrested or indicted; saying, 'that no Londoner ought to go out of the city, but in the highways.' This saying so grieved the Londoners, that suddenly this year a great number of the city assembled themselves in a morning, and a turner, in a fool's coat, came crying through the city, 'Shovels and spades! Shovels and spades!' So many of the people followed, that it was a wonder to behold; and within a short space all the hedges about the city were cast down, and the ditches filled up, and everything made plain, such was the diligence of these workmen.

The fields were never hedged again, but by Stow's time the buildings were spreading inexorably over some of them. A proclamation of Elizabeth's in 1580 forbade any new house within three miles of any London gate, unless an earlier dwelling had stood on the same site within living memory. But neither this proclamation, nor later ones, nor an Act of Parliament, managed to restrain the developers, who knew as many evasive tricks as their descendants in the twentieth century. The Elizabethan attempt to establish a green belt was no more successful than subsequent ones.

Several other modern problems had their counterparts in sixteenth-century London. There was air pollution from the growing use of 'sea-coal', as it was called from its mode of transportation. There was traffic congestion as the first coaches began to lumber through the city, and in the later years of Elizabeth the very fashions of the pedestrians, the hooped skirts, fantastically winged ruffs, and elongated rapiers, caused such obstruction that official action was taken. Men with shears were appointed to snip ruffs and shorten swords that exceeded the authorized measurements. Once the Queen had to apologize to the French ambassador, whose rapier had attracted the attention of these officials, unaware of his diplomatic immunity.

There was, throughout the century, serious inflation caused by the flooding of Europe with gold and silver from the new Spanish conquests in America, and not helped in England by Henry VIII's debasement of the coinage, which Elizabeth had to call in and replace in 1560. In that year five pounds would have bought seventeen and a half yards of cloth, whereas in 1500, in her grandfather's reign, it would have paid for fifty-three. Even so, the inflation continued and in 1600 she lived to see five pounds buying only six yards. The same sum would have bought twenty quarters of wheat in 1500, thirteen and a half in 1530, six and a half in 1560, barely three in 1600.

Nor was the city lacking in violence, fraud, theft, or immorality – and inevitably there were recurrent complaints about the influx of foreigners. The 'Evil May Day' of 1517, really no more than a defiant demonstration by

Henry VIII: bronze medal by Hans Schwartz.

apprentices, with no actual harm to aliens, was taken too seriously by the King and, despite Sir Thomas More's efforts to pour oil on the troubled waters, ended with the hanging of thirteen luckless boys. After Mary's unpopular marriage to Philip of Spain in 1554, 'there was so many Spaniards in London', complained a chronicler, 'that a man should have met in the streets for one Englishman above four Spaniards, to the great discomfort of the English nation.' The Spaniards at least were only birds of passage, as Philip himself was, and many had to occupy temporary accommodation in the halls of the various city companies. Other foreigners settled more permanently, especially the Protestants, known either as Flemings or as Dutchmen, who later fled from Spanish persecution in the Netherlands, and the Huguenots, refugees from the religious wars in France.

Early in Elizabeth's reign she allowed a small number of Jews to enter England and settle in London. They were the first since the expulsion by Edward I and the relaxation seems to have been brief and tentative. Having no separate nationality, these Jews cannot be identified in the census of resident aliens carried out in 1567. The figures show that the 'Dutch' were in a great majority, with 2,030, and the French came next with 428. There were 140 Italians, 45 Spaniards and Portuguese, 44 Burgundians and a mere 40 Scots, who became numerous only after the accession of James I. Twelve years later another census showed a threefold increase in the total of aliens, with the interesting inclusion of 217 negroes and 'Indians', the latter presumably from the New World. Even in Mary's time there had been a wellknown negro in Cheapside who knew the secret of making steel needles, but would not divulge it to the English, who eventually learnt it from a German named Elias Krauss. There was a big rise in the alien population when Antwerp fell to the Spaniards in 1585 and the Duke of Parma expelled all Protestants. It is likely that the official statistics fell far below the real figure. Because of restrictions on trading and employment, many foreigners found it inadvisable to register, and as usual there were plenty of people ready either to shelter them or to exploit them as the case might be. It was a common offence, severely punished when proved, for a Londoner to lend his name to an alien's business or pass off work as his own.

As it turned out, these immigrants – not for the only time in history – made a substantial contribution to the commercial progress of their adopted city. There was Jacopo Verzelini, who took over a vacated friary and manufactured glass in the Venetian manner. Glass of a more ordinary quality, suitable for the windows that were an increasingly important feature of the Tudor house, was made by workers who came over from Lorraine. Starching and starchboiling, so essential for the ruffs and wristbands fashionable with both sexes, were first taught to London women by a Mrs van den Plasse. The plaster ceiling, another distinctive innovation of the period, originally required Italian craftsmen, but those who entered England to work for Henry VIII passed on their skill to native workmen. Foreign visitors might continue to criticize the smug insularity of the Londoners, but the businessmen at least were not too proud to learn from other countries, and if necessary to travel there. Richard Mathews found out how to make the fine tableknives that were a Flemish speciality: soon he was not only making them but had obtained a ban on imports. Richard Dyer travelled through Spain, learnt how to produce portable earthenware stoves, and established his own kiln near Moorgate.

One foreigner who contributed most usefully to London life was Peter Morice, the Dutch servant of Sir Christopher Hatton. The rapid growth of the population had raised problems of water supply. The wells and conduits were inadequate to meet the demand. People were already pumping up river water and storing it in tanks, but it was left to Morice to devise, with all his nation's flair for such engineering, an immense water-wheel built by the first arch of London Bridge, which, Stow tells us,

conveyed Thames water in pipes of lead over the steeple of St Magnus church, at the north end of London Bridge, and from thence into divers men's houses in Thames Street, New Fish Street, and Grass Street, up to the north-west corner of Leadenhall, the highest ground of all the city, where the waste of the main pipe rising into this standard, provided at the charges of the city, with four spouts did at every tide run (according to the covenant) four ways, plentifully serving to the com-modity of the inhabitants near adjoining in their houses, and also cleansed the chan-nels of the street towards Bishopsgate, Aldgate, the bridge, and the Stocks' market.

The ingenious Morice was granted a five-hundred-year lease for his enterprise in 1581 and his descendants held it until 1701. Though that London Bridge and the tidal wheel and the leaden pipes have long vanished, the rights remain as a charge upon the Metropolitan Water Board, which must continue to pay £2·50 annually on each of 1,500 shares to their modern holders until the year 2082.

However flourishing the manufactures of London, and however great the stimulus of ideas and skills from abroad, the city's growth depended pri-marily on its dominant position as a trading centre through which imports and exports flowed. 'It may be called the storehouse and mart of all Europe,' wrote John Lyly in *Euphues and his England* in 1581.

That certainly was the dream of Sir Thomas Gresham, founder of the Royal Exchange, who more than any other individual personifies the age of Tudor enterprise and stands out much as Dick Whittington did in an earlier period.

Gresham was never mayor like his father, Sir Richard, or his uncle, Sir John, both prominent mercers, perhaps because his interests and operations lay more in the international than in the civic sphere. Born in 1519, he went first to Cambridge and then to Gray's Inn, but, students being younger in those days, he was still able to complete an eight-year apprenticeship to his uncle and be admitted to the Mercers' Company in 1543. He then went to the Low Countries, making his headquarters in Antwerp and combining ordinary business with sundry financial commissions for Henry VIII. In this he was following the example of his father, who had earned his knight-hood by negotiating loans from foreign merchants for the King. It was in this field, as a shrewd financial adviser and agent to successive English sovereigns, that young Gresham made his name.

In 1544, now twenty-five, he married. One wonders whether even in this there was not a characteristic element of calculation, for his bride was the

Sixteenth-century bone shoe-horn, inscribed – either as a mark of ownership or by way of advertisement – with the name of Hamlet Radesdale Setteson, 'the Coupar of Londan'.

widow of a London merchant. Three years later, Edward VI came to the throne, a child of nine, and for some time Gresham had to watch the Crown's business in the Low Countries being thoroughly mismanaged by Sir William Dansell. Eventually, in 1551, he was brought in to sort out the muddle, which he did by various ingenious and possibly unscrupulous methods, including the manipulation of the value of sterling on the Antwerp bourse. Edward's Council came to lean on him in other financial perplexities and he was given several diplomatic missions, for which he took no salary but was rewarded with grants of land. All seemed set fair. Then, in July 1553, came the news from Greenwich: the fifteen-year-old King was dead.

Gresham was not the only man whose future was immediately at stake. London was by now a predominantly Protestant city. Mary was the obvious successor to the throne, yet if she succeeded, a devout and dogmatic Catholic, intent on reversing everything that had been done in the past decade, who – and whose interests – would be unaffected?

So, in the first confusion, there was some support for the Duke of Northumberland's desperate scheme to put Lady Jane Grey on the throne. That hapless girl was proclaimed Queen, but the cheers were shaky and an ill-advised vintner's boy shouted 'Long live Queen Mary!' for which indiscretion he had his ears nailed to the pillory. Yet he spoke for the majority, Englishmen preferring legality to theology, and Lady Jane's followers soon melted away. There was an urgent conference in Baynard's Castle, where the late King's Council met with the Lord Mayor and aldermen. Mary was proclaimed Queen and, with her half-sister Elizabeth, given a fulsome welcome to the city. Lady Jane, her relatives and supporters, were clapped into the Tower. About the lad's ears it was too late to do anything.

This turmoil was swiftly followed by Wyatt's rebellion, precipitated by the news that Mary intended to marry Philip of Spain. Once more it was the Kentish men who rose, led by Sir Thomas Wyatt, a swashbuckling soldier of fortune and virulent anti-Spaniard. He marched on London with fifteen thousand sympathizers. Mary, not normally good at public relations, rode from Whitehall Palace to Guildhall, where she was loyally received by the Lord Mayor, Sir Thomas White, and his fellow aldermen, armed for battle. Thousands of citizens volunteered to stand guard round the palace when she returned there.

As usual, the rebels found London Bridge closed against them. As usual, they retaliated by looting part of Southwark. During the night, Wyatt crossed the river at Kingston with the greater part of his force. By two o'clock in the morning he had reached what is now Hyde Park Corner. At Whitehall, where Mary had only five hundred regular troops – the citizens had not yet organized themselves – all was uproar. When the February dawn broke the rebels were all over the modern West End. Their guns were planted on Hay Hill and armed bands were surging round St James's Palace, but Wyatt, no doubt assuming that Mary was in the Tower, pressed on by way of Charing Cross to Ludgate and the city. For most of that short day the street-fighting raged to and fro, and there were times when the news reaching Mary almost convinced her that the battle was lost. But the defenders triumphed in the end, and an exhausted Wyatt was taken prisoner as he sheltered in a fishmonger's near Fleet Street. He duly went to the scaffold, and so – largely because of the fright his rebellion had given Mary – did Lady Jane Grey.

Gresham, of course, was not implicated in these events, but he went into eclipse for a time and his place as financial adviser was taken by a London alderman, William Dauntsey. However, there was clearly nobody like Gresham where money was concerned. Dauntsey was not a great success, and Gresham was restored to royal favour. He could fix foreign loans. When required, he could beat embargoes and blockades, smuggling currency, arms and anything else wanted from abroad. Mary kept him on until she died. Not only were there more grants of land, church land at that, but he was paid twenty shillings a day.

Even so, he probably found Elizabeth a more congenial mistress, especially when, in due course, the outbreak of war in the Low Countries drove him home to London, where he was to spend the rest of his life. He was by now Sir Thomas – she had knighted him before sending him on an embassy – and he had already a firm base in the city. This centred in his plan to establish in London a proper exchange to rival, and now with luck supersede, the bourse at Antwerp with which he was so familiar. Until then, merchants had conducted their dealings in the nave of St Paul's, a rendezvous which they had to share with all kinds of frivolous or disreputable idlers. Gresham offered to build a suitable bourse at his own expense, and the city was glad to provide him with a free site on Cornhill. Its clearance required the removal of eighty houses, but, thanks to the system of frame-construction, it was possible to sell these for dismantling and re-erection elsewhere.

Gresham pushed forward his scheme with characteristic energy. He planned a spacious stone-paved quadrangle, where dealers could move freely in fine weather, and colonnades all round to offer shelter. Everything at ground level was for the wholesalers. The upper galleries were reserved for retail shops, offering the whole range of merchandise, a novelty for Londoners who were still more accustomed to going from street to street to find the various trades. Gresham laid the foundation-stone himself and brought over Flemish bricklayers, thereby provoking a strike among the other workers. Even so, the slates were on the roof within six months, and in due course the final decorations were added, with great golden grasshoppers – Gresham's own emblem – adorning the gatehouse tower, the numerous weather-vanes on the chimneys, and the column that soared triumphantly on the northern side. The day approached when Elizabeth herself would come to visit it.

Here Gresham ran into a difficulty. The lettings for the retail shops upstairs hung fire. It was too new an idea. Traders wondered if they would get their money back. But Gresham was determined to dazzle the Queen with his shopping arcade. He was not going to face the embarrassment of empty shuttered premises. He spent a day personally going round the building and talking to such tenants as were already there. He offered them as many extra shops as they could take over, rent-free for a year, if they would stock them and illuminate them with wax candles for the Queen's visit. Then he made a second circuit of the building that same day, to catch anyone he had missed before and to clinch the bargain with those who had wanted time to consider it.

Ludgate, one of the ten city gates, as rebuilt in 1586. These gates were finally demolished when they strangled the increasing traffic of the eighteenth century.

Overleaf Detail of a panorama by Claes Visscher (1616), showing the Tower and its surroundings, seen from Southwark.

Sixteenth-century woodcut (from the *Roxburghe Ballads*) of a shop interior. Similar premises might have been rented by tenants of Gresham's Royal Exchange.

His enterprise was rewarded. Elizabeth dined with him at his house in Bishopsgate and was then taken on a conducted tour. The retail section, known as 'the Pawn', aroused her special interest, for it was, says Stow, 'richly furnished with all sorts of the finest wares in the city'. So pleased was she that she bade the herald proclaim, with trumpet, that henceforth the building should be known as 'the Royal Exchange'. The retailers were equally satisfied. They remained when their rent-free year was up. Gresham too had cause for content. It was soon possible to raise the rents from forty to ninety shillings a year.

He had the knack of achieving satisfactory solutions. Even for his illegitimate daughter he provided a most presentable husband in Francis Bacon's brother, Sir Nicholas.

His son and heir, however, predeceased him. So, when he himself died of apoplexy in 1579, his fine house in Bishopsgate was left to serve as a college after the death of his widow, with the rents from the Royal Exchange endowing lectureships in divinity, physic, civil law, music and other subjects. In the mornings the lecturers spoke Latin, in the afternoons they were allowed, by a merciful and realistic dispensation, to use English. Today Gresham College survives as the Graduate Business Centre of the City University, and English is the language all day.

The first years of the Royal Exchange coincided with the bitter struggle in the Low Countries. In one way London gained by the decline of Antwerp. In another it was in danger of loss, for English exports had long been too much dependent on the Netherlands market, and the need to find alternative outlets became urgent.

This was the great age of the trading companies, formed by merchants banding themselves together to finance distant voyages and take risks too high for an individual to bear. The Muscovy Company sprang from the expedition of Sir Hugh Willoughby and Richard Chancellor as early as 1553, in a vain attempt to find the North-east Passage to China. Their three little ships dropped down the Thames from Greenwich just as Edward VI lay dying in the palace there, and it was left to Mary, and then Elizabeth, to approve and foster the new commercial relations which developed, really by accident, with Ivan the Terrible. In the 1570s several companies were formed for trade with Turkey and other regions. India and the East Indies beckoned as

London's first shopping centre: the Royal Exchange, built by Sir Thomas Gresham in 1569.

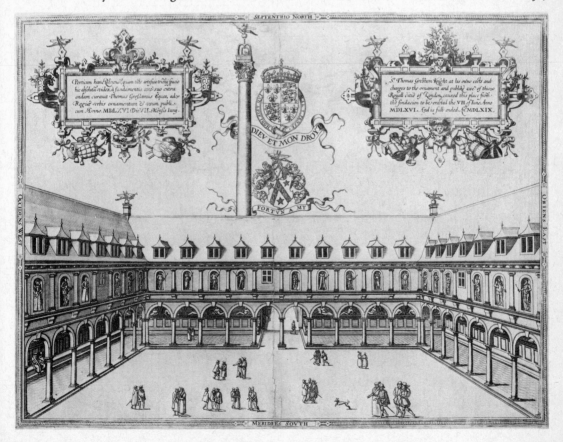

Will:^m Overley Joyner at the Sign of
the East India House *in* Leaden-hall Street LONDON.
Makes all sorts of Sea Chests in Deal or Wainscot,
Ruff or Smooth Packing Chests or Cases, and Cases
of Bottles, & Boxes of all Sizes, Presses in Deal or
Wainscot, & Bedsteds, Tables, Desks, Book Cases, Bu—
rous & Writing Desks, Letter holes, & Drauers for Shops.
Allso Counters and all sorts of Joyners worke done
—— at Reasonable Rates ——

particularly attractive, although remote. Could the Portuguese monopoly be broken there? The market was reconnoitred by a London merchant, Ralph Fitch, who sailed for Aleppo in the *Tiger* – a voyage echoed by the witches in *Macbeth* – and then made an adventurous journey down the Euphrates, Tigris and Persian Gulf, penetrating as far east as Burma. He was away eight years, reappearing in London on 29 April 1591, nineteen days after James Lancaster had sailed from Plymouth with the first English trading expedition to reach India via the Cape. It was the exploratory work of these two men, in their different ways, that led to the formation of the East India Company, which received its charter from Elizabeth on 31 December 1599.

Opposite The old East India House in Leadenhall Street, where subsequently Charles Lamb, a reluctant office-worker from 1792 to 1825, 'made up for coming late by going away early'.

8

'Merry London'

Life, needless to say, was not all earnest industry and commercial endeavour.

'Merry London, my most kindly nurse,' wrote Edmund Spenser. He was born there about 1552, son of a clothworker who had come down from Lancashire, and as a boy he attended the new grammar school of the Merchant Taylors, established in the Duke of Buckingham's old house, pleasantly known as 'the Manor of the Rose', in Suffolk Lane, not far from the river which inspired the refrain of the same poem, 'Sweet Thames! run softly. . . .'

London was still merry in those early years of Elizabeth, and long continued so. There was nothing sudden about the advent of Puritanism or its triumph. Though the word occurs first in Spenser's time, the attitude can be traced far back into the period of supposedly unspoilt 'Merrie England' that used to be idealized by G.K. Chesterton. There had long been conflict between the single-minded businessmen of London and those more frivolous elements likely to seduce their employees from strict attention to work, and the tug-of-war went on, with the city authorities habitually throwing their weight on the side of sobriety. As early as 1418 they had forbidden apprentices and servants to participate in Christmas mumming that involved false beards and make-up, and in 1479 they threatened six days' imprisonment for any 'labourers, servants and apprentices of any artificer or victualler' who played tennis, football, cards or dice. Neither of these prohibitions can be blamed on the Reformation. And neither, probably, was long observed nor did much to

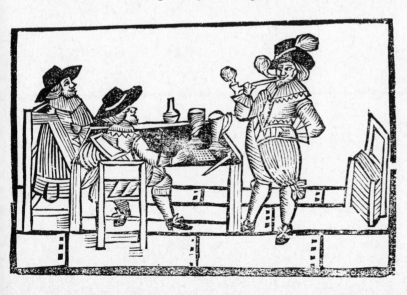

The *Roxburghe Ballads*, a collection of songs and verses, are illustrated with woodcuts that give a vivid impression, if a naïve one, of the lighter side of life in Tudor London. *Opposite* A round dance; *left* a tavern scene.

diminish the pleasures of 'merry London', as Spenser still found it, a century later.

At such times as May Day and Midsummer, especially, the spreading city renewed its ancient rural links and became no more than an overgrown market town. Stow tells of one May morning when Henry VIII 'rode a-may-ing from Greenwich to the high ground of Shooter's Hill' with Catherine of Aragon and a party of courtiers, and how they were met by two hundred archers 'clothed all in green, with green hoods', whose captain, posing as Robin Hood, invited them to a display of marksmanship followed by a picnic of wine and venison served in flower-decked arbours in the woods.

The maypole itself went somewhat into eclipse after the May Day dis-orders of 1517. Traditionally, the chief of these poles had been set up at the junction of Leadenhall Street and St Mary Axe, and was so tall that it dwarfed the adjacent church, which thus came to be known as St Andrew Undershaft. It would have been troublesome to get a new pole of such dimen-sions every spring, and during the year it was hung on iron brackets, extend-ing along the frontages of the neighbouring shops. After 1517 no one ven-tured to erect it again, and in 1549 a zealous preacher at Paul's Cross whipped up the crowd to destroy it as a pagan survival. Stow heard the sermon and described what followed.

Beaufort House, Chelsea, with its formal gardens. This was probably an Elizabethan successor to the mansion in which Sir Thomas More entertained Erasmus and Holbein.

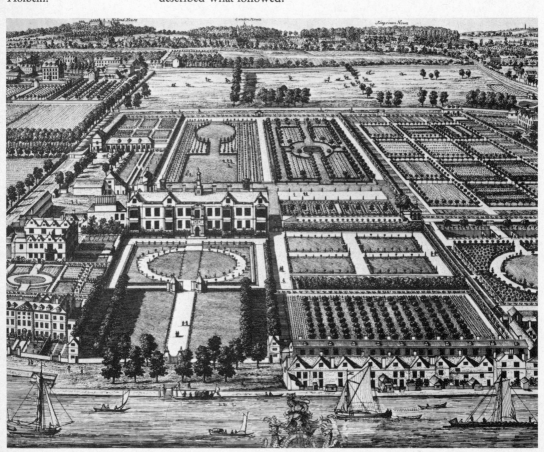

Paul's Cross, near the old St Paul's Cathedral. The open-air pulpit was in some ways the Speakers' Corner of Tudor times. A preacher here, in 1549, incited the crowd to destroy that symbol of pagan fun and games, the maypole.

Such outbursts tended to be local and transitory in their effect. London did not give up its maypoles so easily. The Puritans were ordering their suppres-sion in 1644 and again – significantly – in 1654, and at the Restoration six years later the cheering crowds put back the forbidden emblems as promptly as the royal arms. May Day itself, as a public holiday, even the Common-wealth never managed to abolish: it was still an occasion for Londoners to stroll out in their best clothes, though by that date the fashionable venue had shifted westwards to Hyde Park.

On Midsummer Eve and several other dates, festivals or their vigils, that fell during the summer months, there was a tradition that all the able-bodied townsmen should muster, duly armed and equipped, and parade through the streets. Though these occasions served as a practice mobilization, just as the May Day archery displays had their military value, they were primarily social affairs.

Morris dancer.

Richard Tarlton, Queen
Elizabeth's court jester, the
last in England, and probably
the real-life original of
'Yorick'.

there were usually made bonfires in the streets, every man bestowing wood or labour towards them; the wealthier sort also . . . would set out tables on the vigils, furnished with sweet bread and good drink, and on the festival days with meats and drinks plentifully, whereunto they would invite their neighbours and passengers also to sit and be merry with them in great familiarity, praising God for his benefits bestowed upon them.

Every man's door, he continues, was 'shadowed with green birch, long fennel, St John's wort, orpin, white lilies, and such like, garnished upon with garlands of beautiful flowers. . . .' Glass oil lamps burned all through the short summer night. 'Some hung out branches of iron curiously wrought, containing hundreds of lamps alight at once, which made a goodly show, namely in New Fish Street, Thames Street, etc.'

Besides the 'standing' watch in every ward and street, 'all in bright harness', there was a 'marching watch' of about two thousand men, many of them veteran soldiers, including 'trumpeters on horseback, demilances on great horses, gunners with hand guns . . . archers in coats of white fustian, signed on the breast and back with the arms of the city . . . pikemen in bright corse-lets' and many others, not forgetting the morris dancers. This marching watch paraded through all the main streets, and the bobbing lights of its seven hundred cressets – the invaluable Stow records even the number of them – must have combined with the hanging lamps to turn night into day. What with the mounted trumpeters, the drummers and the fifes, there can have been little chance of sleep, even for those who wanted it.

In this parade, needless to say, the civic heads played a leading part, with 'the mayor himself well mounted on horseback, the swordbearer before him in fair armour well mounted also, the mayor's footmen, and the like torch bearers about him, henchmen twain upon great stirring horses, following him.' The two sheriffs had their separate contingents, lesser but sufficiently impressive, and not omitting 'each their morris dance'. The whole affair grew more and more pompous and expensive, until Henry VIII cancelled the 1539 Midsummer marching watch, following a muster on 8 May which had amounted to fifteen thousand armed citizens. After that, the regular processions lapsed, despite occasional attempts to revive them by Sir John Gresham in Edward VI's reign and by later mayors. The unofficial celebra-tions of Midsummer Eve continued. They must have gladdened Spenser's boyhood with their merriment, just as they furnished Shakespeare with material for the *Dream*. Like the maypole, the Midsummer Watch was too popular to abolish easily. In smaller towns, such as Nottingham, it went on until the Civil War. In London its more serious, military purpose was achieved by parades and exercises ordained by the Privy Council and held in open spaces such as St George's Fields. For entertainment the population began to turn increasingly, as it grew in size, to the more commercialized amusements which a big city could keep regularly on tap. Stow shook his head sadly over the decline of archery in his time, 'giving place to a number of bowling-alleys and dicing-houses, which in all places are increased, and too much frequented.'

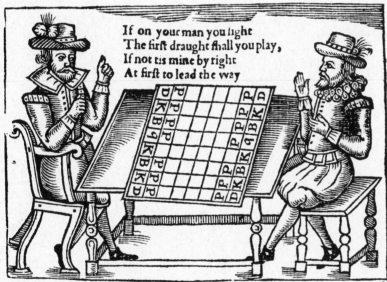

If on your man you light
The first draught shall you play,
If not tis mine by right
At first to lead the way

Bull-baiting and similar savage spectacles had been part of the London
scene ever since anyone could remember. Cheapside itself had once provided
the arena for bulls and mastiffs. Now the city was getting too crowded for such
obstructions and the employers too intolerant of distractions from work and
business. The bull-baiting and bear-baiting accordingly shifted south of the
river, where convenient sites had been left vacant by the dissolution of
Bermondsey Abbey and the Priory of St Mary Overy. The place was handy
for the crowds, yet just outside the jurisdiction of disapproving civic authorities. Sundays and weekdays alike the townsmen streamed across London
Bridge: this misuse of the Sabbath was marked by 'an extraordinary judgment

of God' when a stand collapsed, one Sunday in 1583, causing eight deaths and hundreds of injuries. Criticism of such performances was based rather on their Sabbath-breaking (if held on Sundays) or their threat to production (if held on working days) than on any widespread sympathy for the tormented animals. The Queen herself commanded similar performances at Whitehall and even crossed the river to watch them with her people. And an audience which had just passed under the shrivelled human heads so commonly impaled on London Bridge was not likely to feel squeamish about a gored mastiff or a bleeding bear.

It was in Southwark, too, that the newer amusement and supreme glory of Elizabethan London – the professional theatre – found its principal home.

Drama of one sort or another was nothing new to London. Fitzstephen mentions the religious plays of the twelfth century. The proud guilds of the city were not likely to have been outdone by those of York, Chester, and other towns in the presentation of mystery plays, though unfortunately there is no surviving 'London Cycle' to set against those of the northern fraternities. The schoolboys of Westminster and St Paul's had an early tradition of acting. So had the students of the Inns of Court. All these were amateurs. The first recognized professionals were the actors maintained by kings and noblemen. Henry VII had his *Lusores Regis*, the Players of the King's Interludes, four or five men, later more, who received a retaining fee, were paid additionally for each performance, and were free to accept other engagements in great houses. Cardinal Morton kept his own troupe, and that eminent Londoner Thomas More, when a young man in his household, used to slip on to the stage with them and extemporize. By Henry VIII's time there were, besides the King's Players, the Queen's, the Lord Chamberlain's,

Bankside, looking north across the river. Here was Elizabethan London's amusement centre, with bear-baiting, bull-baiting – and plays. Right of centre stands the Globe, Burbage's original theatre transferred from its site near Finsbury Fields.

The Eell Schipes

THAMESIS

The Bear Gardne

the Marquis of Exeter's and various others. Obviously they could not all be employed full-time in single households and their freedom to act elsewhere increased until they were virtually independent, but the association with a noble patron continued as a legal fiction, since without it they were exposed to the savage legislation against rogues and vagabonds.

Even before Elizabeth's accession, such companies were giving public performances in the courtyards of inns. The Boar's Head in Aldgate was used in 1557 for a presentation of *A Sack Full of News*, a piece so scandalous that it was promptly banned and the actors kept under arrest for twenty-four hours. In future, it was ruled, scripts must be approved by the Church authorities. But this was the last year of Catholic Mary's reign, and dramatic censorship in this form never established itself. The city authorities objected to plays in general, not just to particular themes or phrases. Plays wasted workmen's time, spread infectious diseases, and provided openings for pickpockets and prostitutes. So successive Lord Mayors and aldermen waged continual war, but with only occasional victory, upon those who set up their stages to entertain the citizens.

Other inns used for this purpose were the Bull in Bishopsgate, the Bell and its rival the Cross Keys in Gracious (or Gracechurch) Street, and the Belle Sauvage on Ludgate Hill. The Red Lion at Stepney was putting on plays in 1567. Being outside the city boundary offered immunity from civic interference, an advantage not lost upon James Burbage when he decided to build a special playhouse.

Burbage was just the man for a difficult pioneering venture of this kind. He was not an outstanding actor, but he was in love with his craft and he knew how to draw out the best in others, notably his son Richard as a performer

Richard Burbage: possibly
a self-portrait.

and his subsequent colleague Shakespeare as a writer. Burbage was obstinate,
which was essential. He was also rather unscrupulous, which regrettably
may have been no less vital to his survival. And he had another asset: before
becoming one of the Earl of Leicester's players he had been a joiner, and he
was thus competent, as perhaps no other actor would have been, to design
and build London's first playhouse.

He found a site near Finsbury Fields, outside the Lord Mayor's jurisdiction, and on 13 April 1576 signed a twenty-one-year lease with the clear
proviso that he was free to build a theatre. His father-in-law put up the
money for the work, six or seven hundred pounds. That summer the ex-
joiner ran up a circular building of timber, open to the sky in the middle but
encircled by thatch-roofed galleries, where for twopence – or threepence with a
stool to sit on – patrons could watch in greater comfort than the penny
groundlings standing in the pit. By the autumn Burbage was in business,
presenting not only plays but fencing matches and other attractions. He called
the place simply 'the Theatre', since for the moment there was no other.

This situation did not last long. Within a year the Curtain was built close
by, so called from the curtain wall of the old fortifications. Curtain Road in

Shoreditch still preserves the name. Similar in design, this second playhouse was most likely 'the wooden O' mentioned in *Henry V*. Here both *Romeo and Juliet* and *Every Man in His Humour* first saw the light of day – literally, since performances were usually in the afternoon. A flag was flown when a play was to be acted and trumpets gave warning that it was about to start. Printed playbills were used as early as 1564, even for the inn-yard productions, since the same piece was not given on successive days.

The inns continued to serve as theatres long after the building of the first playhouses. And soon there were more playhouses, attracted to Southwark by that same space and freedom which had already established Bankside as an amusement centre with its bear-baiting, bull-baiting and other rough enter-tainments. Here, on the site of a former rose-garden, Philip Henslowe built the Rose, first of the several theatres he was to own. Henslowe was no dedicated actor like Burbage. He marks the entry of the businessman. He had been apprenticed to a dyer, whose widow he married. His partner in building the Rose was a grocer named John Cholmley. Clearly, whatever the Lord Mayor and aldermen thought of theatres – 'chapels of Satan', the preachers called them – there were individual citizens who preferred to treat them as a sound investment. The Rose opened at Michaelmas, 1587. It was a theatre especially associated with Marlowe's plays and with the actor Edward Alleyn, who, by marrying his manager's stepdaughter, eventually inherited Henslowe's substantial property interests. These with his own accumulation – he was the son of a prosperous London innkeeper, besides becoming the foremost actor of his day – enabled him to endow Dulwich College in 1619 and indirectly its Victorian offshoot, Alleyn's School.

Another worthy citizen, Francis Langley, built the Swan in 1596, braving the open opposition of the Lord Mayor. This too stood on Bankside in the 'Paris' (or Parish) Garden not far from the Bear Gardens. It was close to the river, accessible by several landing-stages or 'stairs' as they were called, and is

Edward Alleyn, actor and businessman.

Coaches, introduced early in Elizabeth's reign and originally for use in the country, soon multiplied in London, causing traffic problems and threatening the livelihood of the watermen.

thought to have owed its name to the swans that were a common sight in the vicinity. A Dutch visitor, John de Witt from Utrecht, thought this 'the largest and most distinguished' of the theatres, 'since it contains three thousand persons' (probably a high but not absurd estimate) 'and is built of a concrete of flint stones (which greatly abound in Britain) and supported by wooden columns in such exact imitation of marble that it might deceive even the most cunning.' These architectural splendours were not quite matched by the subsequent history of the Swan. In its second year the production of a seditious comedy entitled *The Isle of Dogs* led to the temporary closure of all theatres and the imprisonment of the author and cast concerned, while in 1600 an enterprising impresario named Richard Vennar announced a spectacular entertainment called *England's Joy* and, having secured a full house, vanished with the takings and left a far from joyful audience to relieve their feelings by wrecking the theatre.

The business arrangements varied with the managements. Henslowe has been described as a capitalist, employing and arguably exploiting the players. Burbage on the other hand believed in a co-operative system. Permanent members of the company were 'sharers'. Shakespeare was one such sharer, and achieved his prosperity thereby, not as a playwright, for each play brought him only a modest once-for-all payment. The boys who took the female parts were usually apprenticed to one or other of the leading actors. There was thus a rough-and-ready correspondence with the guild system of the recognized trades. Minor members of the cast, who had not achieved the status of sharers, formed an intermediate category like the journeymen in any other craft.

There was one drawback to Burbage's design for the Theatre: the absence of a roof over stage and pit made such buildings unattractive in the winter. So, in 1597, the last year of his life, he managed to buy part of the old Blackfriars monastery. Already, since the Dissolution, the place had been used for theatrical performances, first by the Master of the Revels and then by those companies of child actors whose competition so much incensed the adult professionals. But now these lisping players had vacated the building and Burbage's company moved in. Their new auditorium was lit by candles, there were benches for the pit and stools in the several galleries, and for all this luxury the admission charges were correspondingly higher. It was probably here that Shakespeare, within the next two or three years, played Adam in his own *As You Like It* and the Ghost in *Hamlet*.

James Burbage, however, died in the year he acquired this indoor theatre. That was also the twenty-first and last year of the lease for the original playhouse. The ground landlord had previously been awkward, forcing Burbage to find another ten pounds rent, a serious addition to the overheads. Now he gave notice to Burbage's sons that he would not renew the lease. But even in death the ex-joiner had the last laugh, for, the building being all of timber, Cuthbert Burbage was able to dismantle and re-erect it on Bankside, where, renamed the Globe, it provided the stage for his brother Richard's triumphs in so many of Shakespeare's subsequent plays.

No doubt it would have irritated many respectable Elizabethan Londoners if they could have foreseen that, four centuries later, posterity would remember

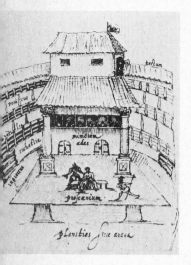

Interior of the Swan Theatre. This is a contemporary copy of a drawing (now lost) with which John de Witt illustrated his description.

Ben Jonson: portrait by an unknown artist. Born in Westminster, a stormy and controversial figure, he did more perhaps than Shakespeare to reflect the London life of their time.

their proud city with such disproportionate emphasis on an aspect they would have dismissed as trivial and dubious. Yet, when almost every material trace of that city has vanished, it is the heritage of drama that survives and interests the whole of the literate world. And, incidentally, it is in those plays – not so much Shakespeare's perhaps, but Ben Jonson's *Bartholomew Fair*, Beaumont and Fletcher's *Knight of the Burning Pestle*, and many others – that the life of London in late Elizabethan and early Jacobean times is more faithfully preserved for us than in any other form.

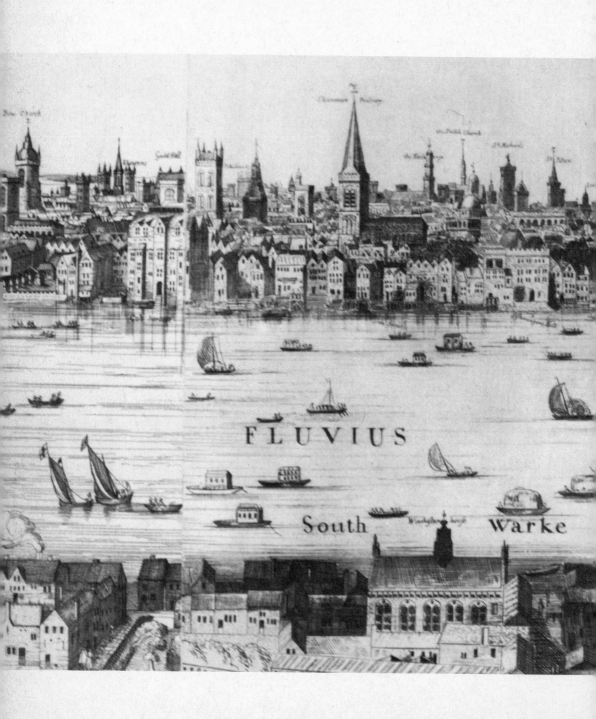

FLUVIUS

South Warke

9

The Key to the Kingdom

For half a century Elizabeth had charmed the Londoners. They had loved her first as the captive princess. When, after the collapse of Wyatt's rebellion, Mary had sent her by river from the Tower to Richmond, the merchants along the waterfront had cheered her passing barge and fired off gun-salutes. That popularity had lasted, despite all her deviousness and delays, her maddening manoeuvres and her notorious parsimony, right into her last decade as a tired old woman. Even glamorous Essex, galloping along Cheapside in 1601 with his insurgent band, had failed to rouse the citizens against her imperfect government.

'She kept them bewitched,' says her modern biographer, Sir John Neale, 'for it was a secret of power to hold this key to the kingdom.' It was a secret James I never grasped. Nor did Charles I, who lost kingdom and head in consequence.

London showed little enthusiasm for the Stuart strangers when they came south in 1603. The succession was an unforeseen, unwelcome consequence of that marriage exactly a century before, which Dunbar's diplomacy had helped to arrange. James's unchallenged coming preserved the peace: that was all that could be said. Before he was proclaimed, there was republican talk in the Privy Council. Ralegh is said to have advised, 'Let us keep the staff in our own hands, and set up a commonwealth.' Or at least, he urged, impose terms on the newcomer. Set a limit on the number of Scots he may bring. This bold suggestion found no support. James, a dogmatic believer in the divine right of kings, was not the man to tolerate such negotiations. He came south with the expected entourage of parasites. Two years later Guy Fawkes was asked why he was guarding a ton and a half of gunpowder in a vault beneath the House of Lords. His answer must have earned the unspoken sympathy of some among his interrogators: 'One of my objects was to blow Scotchmen back into Scotland.'

The natural curiosity of the Londoners to see their new monarch was frustrated by the plague of that summer in 1603, which prevented the traditional eve-of-coronation procession from the Tower to Westminster. Ben Jonson's programme of street pageants was cancelled. Only the Lord Mayor and twelve aldermen were given places at the ceremony in the Abbey, and all other Londoners were banned from entering Westminster for fear of spreading the contagion. James made no subsequent effort to compensate them for their disappointment. When not away hunting – in which pastime he seems to have been more of a butcher than a sportsman – he liked to isolate himself in his favourite palace of Whitehall, where he turned the Court into a more-than-usually enclosed society with a bias towards hard

Elizabeth I: a silver medal commemorating the defeat of the Spanish Armada in 1588. For half a century she charmed the Londoners.

Opposite Detail from Hollar's panoramic view of the London skyline. The spire of St Laurence Poultney is prominent in the centre.

The Gunpowder Plot: the public execution of Guy Fawkes and his fellow conspirators outside the Parliament House.

drinking and homosexuality, so that before long the Queen set up her own household at Denmark House. He had no desire to see his subjects and was frankly puzzled that they should want to see him. When a courtier tried to explain that these good folk only wished to look upon his face, he lost his temper and burst out, with characteristic delicacy, 'God's wounds! I will pull down my breeches and they shall also see my arse!'

It must be admitted in fairness that this unattractive monarch did something for the welfare of the Londoners he despised. In late Elizabethan times a scheme had been mooted to bring much-needed drinking water to the city along a channel cut across country from Hertfordshire. The first promoter, Edmund Colthurst of Bath, gave up through lack of capital in 1605. After a few years the New River scheme was revived by Hugh Myddleton, a Basinghall Street goldsmith of Welsh origin and a typical speculator of the period, whose diversified interests included silver-mining in Cardiganshire, land-reclamation in the Isle of Wight, and Ralegh's semi-piratical activities on the Spanish Main.

The New River was, for those days, a considerable engineering project. A force of 130 labourers had to dig a channel ten feet wide and four feet deep for over thirty-eight miles to end in a great reservoir at Clerkenwell, whence the water would be piped to subscribing householders through hollowed elm-trunks with iron collars at the joints. The over-all length of the channel was originally still greater, since in places it had to take a winding course, not so

much because of the lie of the land as to reduce the opposition of the individual landowners. Eight hundred bridges were required to preserve the rights of way. Myddleton was in fact encountering the problem faced by the railway pioneers more than two centuries later, that of finding the shortest and straightest way to the outskirts of London despite the determined hostility of those whose property was affected.

Myddleton was not without influence. His brother Thomas was soon to be Lord Mayor. He himself was an alderman and M.P. for his native town of Denbigh – though Parliamentary connections were naturally less relevant in those days to a local scheme of this type. But it was King James whose interest proved decisive. He expressed concern for the 'poor people enforced to use foul and unwholesome water' and put his own money into the venture when some of Myddleton's city backers began to desert him. With the King involved, opposition was muted. In 1613 there was an official opening at the reservoir, the New River Head, fittingly on the September day when his brother was nominated as the next Lord Mayor. Six years later the New River Company was formed, with Hugh Myddleton as its first governor and with 'adventurers' shares' like those in the East India, Muscovy, and other more exotic companies of the day. James was a shareholder himself. In 1631 his less commercially minded son exchanged the shares for an annuity of £500, known as the King's Clog, which is still paid to the Crown by the Metropolitan Water Board.

The Waterhouse at the New River Head, Islington. James I took shares in Hugh Myddleton's ambitious project.

Golden head of a ceremonial mace of the Mercers' Company, 1679.

The completion of 'Sir Hugh Myddleton's Glory' was particularly welcome since the growth of the city continued, unabated by renewed proclamations against new building. The tendency in James's time, and thereafter, was for London to spread westwards. Apart from the lack of space in the old city there were many families who preferred to exchange their houses there for new homes in what is now the West End. A new snobbery was beginning to develop. For the first time we hear of noblemen and gentlefolk disliking the proximity of men 'in trade'. Smoke too had long been a nuisance, and, though it was complained of even at Westminster, the prevailing westerly winds made that side of the city preferable. Traffic also had vastly increased. As a character observes in Dekker's comedy, *The Roaring Girl*, in 1610, 'They keep a vile swaggering in coaches nowadays; the highways are stopped with them.' And in 1623 the waterman poet, John Taylor, mouthpiece of the countless boatmen plying for hire, was lamenting that 'all our profit runs away on wheels'. He exaggerated, but there had certainly been a phenomenal increase in coaches since their first appearance in the streets less than seventy years earlier. What Taylor complained of was the number of hackney coaches as well as private vehicles. Stage-coaches were not in use until about 1650, but stage-wagons, rumbling along at a snail's pace, were already clogging the entrances of the city. And now there were sedan chairs adding to the obstruction. No wonder that, for one reason or another, there was a move towards the open spaces to the west. Piccadilly, the 'way to Reading', acquired its name about 1627, as more and more houses sprang up along the roadside. It was taken from Piccadilly Hall, built in 1611 near today's Great Windmill Street. Its owner was a retired tradesman, Robert Baker, who had made his money from 'piccadills', the ruffs and collars then fashionable.

The sites along the Strand were now finally taken up. The last of the great houses, Northumberland House as it became in 1642, was originally built for the Earl of Northampton in 1605 to the designs of Bernard Jansen and Gerard Christmas. It stood where there had been a convent in Catholic times, and where now Northumberland Avenue runs down to the river. For other new mansions the builders had to seek sites elsewhere. In 1607 Sir Walter Cope commissioned John Thorpe to build for him, right out in Kensington, what was later to be known as Holland House and might have survived uniquely to this day, but for the incendiary bombs of 1941 which spared only the east wing. The associations of Holland House are not confined to the great period when its owner, nephew of Charles James Fox, made it the centre of Whig society. When the first Earl of Holland was executed in 1649, two Parliamentary generals, Fairfax and Lambert, occupied it. William Penn lived there, William and Mary found temporary quarters under its roof in 1689, and Addison made it his home for the last three years of his life.

Holland House would have seemed remote to many in James's time. The trouble was that most of the nearest land stretching west of the town belonged to one or other of several great landowners, and even when they wished to develop it they met with opposition. Thus, there were still fields with cows grazing on the western side of St Martin's Lane. These belonged to the Lord

The Roaring Girle.

OR
Moll Cut-Purse.

As it hath lately beene Acted on the Fortune-stage by
the Prince his Players.

Written by *T. Middleton* and *T. Dekkar*.

My cafe is alter'd, I muft worke for my liuing.

. Printed at *London* for *Thomas Archer*, and are to be fold at his
fhop in Popes head-pallace, neere the Royall
Exchange. 1611.

Title-page of *The Roaring Girl* ('written by T. Middleton and T. Dekkar', but probably mostly by Dekker). Even as early as this, London's traffic jams were commented on.

Treasurer, the Earl of Salisbury, as one street-name, Cecil Court, still reminds us. He built houses on them, thereby annoying not only the adjacent
cottagers but also his sovereign, since the consequent drainage ditch caused
flooding in the Palace of Whitehall.

123

1: Westminster Abby. 2: Westminster Hall. 3: St James's Palace. 4: Pell mall. 5: Conduit.

Above St James's Palace (right of this picture) and Westminster Abbey (centre) as they appeared in 1660. To the left is Westminster Hall. In the foreground stands a conduit, and the road behind it is Pall Mall.

Right Sir Paul Pindar, a wealthy merchant and sometime ambassador to Constantinople, built his house in Bishopsgate. This print of 1812 shows it in its latter days as a public house, 'The Paul Pindar'.

Opposite Northumberland House, where Northumberland Avenue runs today. Built in 1605, it survived into Victoria's reign.

Arundel House (north view *above*, south view *below*), the town house of Thomas Howard, 2nd Earl of Arundel, was one of the great houses of the Strand. It stood on the site of what is now Arundel Street.

Immediately to the west lay the Lammas Fields owned by the Earl of Leicester, who early in Charles I's reign tried to develop the site. Popular outcry led to a Privy Council inquiry, which permitted him only to build a house for himself at one side. The hope was to keep the rest as an open space, but further development came after the Restoration, and now only Leicester Square preserves, on a small scale, the original intention.

Another earl, Bedford, owned the former monastic property, Covent Garden, on Salisbury's other side. Here in 1632 Inigo Jones laid out his italianate piazza, the most remarkable single scheme of all this period. The fruit and vegetable market so famous in later years began as a mere incidental convenience for the owners of the fine new houses standing round.

Lincoln's Inn Fields saw the last of these big schemes before the interruption of the Civil War. In 1638 a Bedfordshire builder, William Newton, produced a plan to erect thirty-two houses between High Holborn and Drury Lane. It was not cottagers now but lawyers who rose in protest. Though presumably more influential and articulate, they were no luckier. The houses went up and others followed. What had been a great expanse of open land, which the lawyers would have liked to see laid out with walks for public recreation, shrank to its present size. None the less, Lincoln's Inn Fields claims to be the biggest square in central London, and the aim of public recreation, seem to be fulfilled, especially during the lunch-hour on a fine day.

Inigo Jones was not directly involved in all these developments. Indeed, versatile and indefatigable as 'the English Palladio' proved himself, he can scarcely have designed and built everything that has been attributed to him, let alone what has not. But his influence was incalculable, and early Stuart London bore his individual stamp as unmistakably as the late Stuart city carried that of Wren.

Jones came to his position in an oddly indirect way. Like Ben Jonson, with whom he was to collaborate and quarrel, he was a humbly born Londoner. His early talent for drawing attracted a nobleman's patronage and sent him on his first continental travels, which had brought him, by the time of James's accession, to Denmark. The King there was James's brother-in-law. So it was that the son of a Welsh clothworker in Smithfield reached Whitehall through an introduction from the Danish court.

Lincoln's Inn Fields, from the north-west. This was the last of the big development schemes – and one that was hotly opposed – before the interruption of the Civil War.

Set design by Inigo Jones for Ben Jonson's masque *Oberon* (1611).

For a long time he was known chiefly as a theatrical designer. It is said that Anne of Denmark, having an imperfect knowledge of English, preferred spectacle to the subtler verbal displays that the quicker-witted Elizabeth had been able to appreciate. James, though intellectual enough, had also a leaning towards the masque, finding in its stately splendours all kinds of comforting symbolism to accord with his mystical view of royalty. Certainly, though plenty of drama continued to be acted – Shakespeare and his colleagues appeared on numerous occasions at Whitehall – the masques became increasingly fashionable. They called for artificial lighting and for elaborate 'engines' and 'devices' to secure magical effects, in all of which Jones excelled. Court fashion quickly found its reflection in the popular playhouse, and the open-air theatres gave place to covered ones lit by candles and lending themselves to illusion. One such was converted out of a cock-pit in Drury Lane, which was roofed over for the purpose in 1616. It was burnt down on Shrove Tuesday the following year, in the boisterous merrymaking with which the apprentices celebrated that day, but it was quickly rebuilt as the Phoenix Theatre.

By that time Inigo Jones was displaying his genius on a wider stage. In 1615, after another protracted tour of the Continent, he was appointed surveyor of the royal buildings and his architectural vision, inspired by all he had just seen in Italy, was paired with James's ambitions for his capital. The King quoted Suetonius's comment on the Emperor Augustus, that he had found Rome a city of brick and left it one of marble. James would be happy enough to boast that 'we had found our city and suburbs of London of sticks, and left them of brick'. For the Palace of Whitehall he planned a particularly magnificent transformation. It would be pulled down and completely rebuilt as the most superb royal residence in Europe. To judge from the designs prepared by Inigo Jones and his nephew, John Webb, it would have been, but we have only the Banqueting House, built in 1619, as a sample. James's aspirations always outran his means. He had inherited England as a penniless Scots cousin, and never grasped that the dazzling legacy was limited. Nevertheless, though the new Whitehall remained an unfulfilled dream, Jones had his chance elsewhere. From the building of the Queen's House at Greenwich in 1617 he was constantly busy, in London and outside, until his loyalty to the Stuarts brought his career to an abrupt end in 1642.

In 1617 James issued a curious edict, repeated by Charles in 1632, that gentlemen who did not own a town house should quit London and live on their estates in the country. Whatever the object of this decree, it had two alternative effects on the social life of the capital. Where it was accepted without demur, it increased the already notorious isolation of the Court and eventually pushed many of the best families into the anti-Royalist camp. For the first time since the Wars of the Roses there had appeared in the House of Lords, after James's accession, a powerful group opposed to the reigning monarch. As Shakespeare's patron, the outspoken Earl of Southampton, complained, 'I like not to come to the council board, because there are so many boys and base fellows there.' Needless to say, James made himself equally numerous enemies in the Commons. By banishing many of that class to their homes in the provinces, he still further contracted his Court and cut himself off from his subjects. On the other hand, there were some gentlemen unwilling to lose their foothold in London, and these, if they had no town house, hastened to acquire one. This may have fitted in with James's schemes for a more impressive capital. Though he might discourage the unplanned growth of workaday London, he could scarcely object to some additional residences for the quality.

Having managed to alienate so large a section of the English aristocracy and gentry, James had no difficulty in offending the London merchants, whose independent philosophy of life conflicted with his own dogma of the divinity that hedged a king. There was a revealing incident in 1617, when James, no sabbatarian, clashed with the Puritans then ascendant in the city. The Lord Mayor refused leave for the royal coaches to pass through the streets during the hours of divine service. James exploded. 'Two kings cannot reign in the same kingdom,' he informed the Lord Mayor. That officer stood his ground. True, he admitted respectfully, but there was a King even higher than James, and it was His will that must be obeyed. The dispute ended in compromise: the coaches were allowed to pass, but only on condition that James did not set a bad example by riding in one of them.

James I and his Queen, Anne of Denmark. The King's way of life in London soon provoked her into establishing a separate household.

Things were really no better when Charles succeeded his father in 1625. Symbolically, a thunderstorm and downpour marred his ceremonial return to London with his bride, Henrietta Maria, whom he brought up from Green-wich to Somerset House by state barge with a fine flotilla of escorting craft. The Londoners lined the banks loyally enough. After the vulgarity and debauchery of the late King, drooling over his 'sweet Steenie', the hated Duke of Buckingham, they had hopes of this dignified and decent young man and the attractive young girl (though unfortunately French) with whom he was to share his throne. They made a striking couple standing in the barge, both in green velvet with gold embroidery, Charles with a broad-brimmed black felt hat, sporting a red plume, and Henrietta Maria with a grey one and white feathers. But, though it was June, fierce hail rattled down on the unprotected crowds, and to cap everything several overladen boats and rafts turned over, throwing scores of people into the water, fortunately without any fatalities. Still, it was typical. In London few things went right for the Stuarts.

Charles I dining in public –
he was evidently a more
accessible monarch than his
father, or had a slightly
better understanding of public
relations.

The Queen had brought over an immense entourage of her own country-
men, including a bishop and more than thirty Catholic priests. They filled
Somerset House – the original Somerset House built for the Lord Protector in
1547, an appropriately Frenchified mansion modelled on the Château
d'Ecouen. In small ways and big, these newcomers upset the citizens, as
when Madame de St Georges, the Queen's bosom friend, threw her English
breakfast out of the window into the Strand. Crowds gathered in the street,
howling, 'Death to the French Papists!' and others picketed the river frontage
in boats, voicing the same sentiments. For once, Charles sided with his
subjects. He gave Buckingham the unpleasant job of clearing out the whole
party and packing them off to France.

The coronation in February was fraught with controversy and ill omen. It
was judged wisest to omit the state progress, as in James's case, using the
same excuse of the plague. Henrietta quarrelled violently with her devoted
bridegroom. She refused to be crowned by a Protestant heretic and did not
even attend the ceremony. And when, at the crucial moment, the Earl of
Arundel called on the congregation to acknowledge Charles as their rightful
King, there was an embarrassing silence. Charles left the Abbey in tears.
What should, in a special sense, have been 'his' day was emphatically not. To
cap everything, there was an alarming earth tremor early in the afternoon.

The times were in any case difficult. The closing years of James had seen war in Germany and the Low Countries which had hit the cloth trade hard, with more general economic repercussions lasting throughout Charles's life. He himself was immediately at odds with Parliament, which was grudging in voting him subsidies. From 1629 to 1640 he did not call Parliament at all.

In 1636 he fell out with the City over some technical infractions of the Londonderry charter. Under this, the confiscated O'Neill lands in Ireland had been handed over to the livery companies for development, a colonizing venture that had brought scant benefit to the merchants and saddled the town of Derry with an official name still hotly controversial. Charles instituted a Star Chamber case against the Common Council. It incurred a fine of £70,000, subsequently reduced to £12,000. The City paid up. Charles, though chronically short of money, handed the whole sum to Henrietta Maria as a birthday present. A year later he was asking the City for a loan. He was hurt and puzzled when it was not forthcoming.

So, inexorably, the King moved to his doom. He made that incomparable, that never-to-be-too-much-lamented collection of art treasures which it took Cromwell almost three years to disperse on the international market. He lived in a world hardly less unreal than those elaborately contrived masques in which he himself sometimes performed. And, while intently watching his step upon the stage, he continued clumsy in the more vital manoeuvres of statecraft and gave no thought to the key to his kingdom, that restless city beyond the peaceful bowling green he had made himself at Charing Cross.

His friend Strafford, 'Black Tom', was more alive to political realities. When the Common Council refused Charles his loan, the Earl commented

The original Somerset House, built in 1547, was modelled on the Château d'Ecouen; it was thus an appropriate dwelling for Queen Henrietta Maria's French retinue.

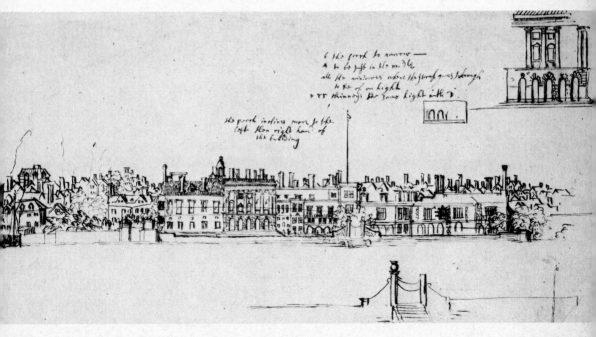

1 You ar to accuse thofe ~~???~~ joint lie & feueralie

2 you ar to referue the power of making additionally

3 When the Comitie for examination is a naming (wch you must prefs to be clofe & under tey of feeresie) if eather Efsex, Warwick, Holland, Say, ~~????~~ Wharton, or Brooke be named, you must defyre that they may be spared becaufe you ar to examine them as witnefses for me

Charles R

Instruction in King Charles I's own hand to the Attorney-General concerning the impeachment of the 'five Members' – or six including Lord Kimbolton.

bluntly, 'Unless you hang up some of them, you will do no good with them.' Strafford was at least consistent, however unwise. When his autocratic behaviour provoked the apprentices to riot in 1640, he had two of them promptly hanged, one after torture. But against Strafford was ranged another strong man, 'King' Pym, the great Parliamentarian, who could bring out the Londoners on to the streets at will. That year ten thousand citizens put their names to his petition, demanding that a Parliament be called again. Charles yielded. After a gap of eleven years Westminster hummed again as the lords and lawyers and country squires came riding in from every corner of the kingdom. It was about this time that, according to tradition, Henrietta Maria gave the opposition the nickname that was to stick. With Charles she had to make her way through a vast concourse of Puritans, estimated at twenty thousand, each waving a paper inscribed with the word *Liberty*. In that throng of soberly dressed, crop-haired demonstrators one youth took her fancy, and she cried out gaily, 'See what a handsome roundhead!'

The next year or two saw the drift to disaster which is English, not London, history. But London was the main setting and the role of the Londoners was decisive. Strafford was duly impeached and sentenced by law, but it was the menace of the mob, demanding the execution of 'Black Tom, the tyrant', that frightened Charles into signing his friend's death-warrant. Only when the Queen herself was threatened did he nerve himself for resistance. Everyone is familiar with the scene in the Commons on 4 January 1642, when he burst in to arrest the famous 'Five Members', Pym, Hampden and the others. Not all remember the sequel, when Charles, observing that 'the birds had flown' and suspecting that they were 'lurking in the City', went down to Guildhall and demanded that the Common Council hand them over. He had a mixed reception. The Lord Mayor, Sir Richard Gurney, was a royalist and there were many of those responsible civic leaders who flinched from defying their sovereign. But Pym's followers had won a majority in the elections to the Common Council only a few weeks before, so Charles failed at Guildhall as he had failed in the House of Commons.

He had lost the key to the kingdom. He had no military force adequate to impose his will on the citizens. Within the week, on 10 January, he quitted his capital. He never returned except as a prisoner.

From January until August, when he raised his standard at Nottingham and the Civil War began, there were some months of moving and counter-moving, as the two parties closed their ranks and tried to make sure, up and down the country, of strategic positions and ammunition stores. Charles wrote to the Lord Mayor. The citizens must not comply with Parliament's demands to raise men, money and arms against him. Gurney posted his order, as a proclamation, in all the usual public places throughout the city. Parliament struck back. Gurney was relieved of his office and sent to the Tower. It was a blow to local liberties, an infringement of the city's dignity, but the Londoners were in a dilemma between two national authorities greater than themselves, and they were more willing to tolerate the interference of Parliament.

The fighting started. Edgehill, though inconclusive, was a royalist success in that it left Charles free to advance upon his disobedient capital. He might have won the war then. He lost it when the Londoners, massed in their trained bands, marched out to confront him at Turnham Green. The Cavaliers were outnumbered two to one, and after an exchange of cannon-fire they retreated.

In earlier years, like the Home Guard of our own century, the trained bands had often been good for a joke. They had been uproariously guyed on the stage in *The Knight of the Burning Pestle*. Since 1616 they had been organized in four regiments, representing the north, south, east and west quarters of

A woodcut from a Civil War pamphlet shows 'the Resolution of the women of London, wherein they declare their hot zeale in sending their husbands to the Warres'.

London, under the command of the Lord Mayor, and now at the outbreak of the Civil War they were quickly expanded into nine regiments and five auxiliary units, making a total of over sixteen thousand men. They were mostly musketeers or pikemen, but the Honourable Artillery Company, chartered by Henry VIII in 1537 as a 'Guild of Archers and Handgunmen' and still in very proud existence to this day, provided an *élite* responsible for the training and leadership of the whole force. This was about the time that Milton, then living in Aldersgate Street, was enrolled in the Company and wrote his sonnet 'When the Assault was intended to the City'. It was the trained bands, no joke now but a formidable fighting force, who not only held London but later marched across country to raise the siege of Gloucester, and on their way home demonstrated at the first Battle of Newbury that they could hold their own against an equal number of Cavaliers in the open field.

It was in vain that Charles tried to recover London. In January 1643 he ordered a blockade of the city, banning all communication with it and in particular cutting off its supply of sea-coal from Newcastle, which he held. It proved to be a hard winter. Short of fuel in their homes, the townspeople congregated round street-corner bonfires, keeping themselves warm with lusty psalm-singing and (we may hope) deriving comfort from the inflammatory speeches of the agitators. Morale at this stage was, high. The very building of the city's defences had brought everyone together. In his *Survey of London*, published that year, William Lithgow paints a vivid word-picture of the trained bands marching out with flying colours and beat of drum, shouldering their mattocks and shovels instead of muskets and pikes, while the women, carrying wicker baskets to shift the earth, formed themselves into orderly columns in imitation of the men. These ramparts met the river well upstream from the 'Horse Ferry' that has left its name to the modern road. From what is now Pimlico the line ran round the north of London to reach the Thames again at Wapping. Then, on the south, it zigzagged from Rotherhithe to Vauxhall. In all, it extended eighteen miles, with twenty-four forts. These defences were never tested. The royal strategy for 1643 provided for three armies to converge on the capital, but the plan never came to anything.

This is not to say that London felt no hardships or that opposition to Charles was unanimous. There was much unemployment in the city, the shops were empty of goods, the unsettled conditions at sea allowed few vessels to keep foreign trade going. The women, impatient of ideological arguments, clamoured for an end to the struggle. In August that year two hundred of them started one morning from Clerkenwell with a petition to the House of Commons, demanding peace and the return of the King. Perhaps it was not an entirely spontaneous demonstration: it is said that there were thirty or forty men disguised among them. At all events, by the time they reached Palace Yard their numbers had increased to four thousand, and their forcible dispersal by the trained bands caused wild disorder and serious casualties. The incident encouraged Charles to write to the Lord Mayor from his Oxford headquarters, voicing his desire 'to see the country once more settled and at peace'. But Parliament would permit no weakening, and when the Lord Mayor published the letter he was arrested for his pains.

A Royalist plot in 1643 involved arresting Pym, Hampden and other prominent Parliamentarians, and capturing arsenals, magazines and similar strategic points. This detail from a contemporary broadsheet shows forts and outworks of the Tower which were to be occupied 'to prevent all supplies'. The plot failed.

The trial of King Charles I in Westminster Hall.

The King returned, but not until that bleak January of 1649, when the final scenes of the tragedy were enacted: the solemn trial in Westminster Hall, the last night of the condemned man in St James's Palace, the walk across the park, through the gallery that then spanned the road through Whitehall like a bridge, and along more galleries to Inigo Jones's banqueting house, where a little of the wall had been specially demolished for easy access to the scaffold raised outside. Pepys, then a schoolboy at St Paul's, was in the crowd gathered to see the axe fall.

For the next eleven years London was the capital of a Commonwealth. To the man in the street the victory tasted sour. Even the most righteous war has to be paid for, and London found itself asked for money as in former days. When it was not collected promptly enough, whole regiments of unpaid troops were billeted on the householders, while from the wealthy merchants, goldsmiths and others, there were heavy confiscations. As if the inevitable hardships and shortages were not enough, the Puritan zealots (of whom Cromwell himself was certainly not one) did their best to stamp on the traditional amusements which had enlivened early periods even when matters were at their worst. The playhouses had been closed at the outbreak of war. Even the churchgoer was starved of music and spectacle, as the organs were removed, the choirs disbanded, and even anything so mildly decorative as a surplice forbidden. The maypole and all its innocent gaieties, long frowned on, were now discontinued by official order, and on Christmas Eve, 1652, a killjoy House of Commons excelled itself by abolishing Christmas Day.

A satirical Dutch print shows Cromwell dismissing the Rump parliament ('you have sate long enough'), while in the background Harrison lays violent hands on Mr Speaker.

Cromwell, for all his doings in Ireland, was a more tolerant man. It is significant that it was under his regime that the Jews were allowed back in London after centuries of exclusion. They settled at first round Petticoat Lane. They were Sephardic Jews, previously associated with Spain and Portugal. The more numerous Jews who came to London in later times were of the Ashkenazim community from Germany, Poland and Russia: their immigration began as early as William of Orange's reign, but was vastly increased by the pogroms of Tsarist Russia and the more systematic persecutions of Nazi Germany.

Cromwell's well-intentioned reforms probably meant less to the average Londoner than his own immediate grievances and the evidence, however misleading, of his eyes. It seemed to him odd that Cromwell, having killed the anointed King, should install himself in Whitehall, surrounded with royal pomp. It is easier, with hindsight, to imagine that Cromwell, a moderate man in a desperate and responsible position, bedevilled with the disunity and unrealistic dogmas of the smaller men around him, was forced to behave like an autocrat. In fairness it must be remembered that he was offered the title of king and refused it. But, if he was to exercise personal power and be respected, in the only way that the seventeenth-century citizen would understand, he must look the part, as even a Lord Mayor must. So, for his closing years, he moved into the palace, was addressed as 'Highness', and retained most of the old court etiquette, though he changed the scarlet-and-gold uniform of the Yeomen of the Guard to a more sober grey-and-silver – and, needless to say, was criticized for that too. One of his first engagements as Lord Protector was on 8 February 1654, when he drove in state to a City banquet at Grocers' Hall. He was welcomed at Temple Bar with a speech from the Recorder, there was a gun-salute from the Tower and a presentation of plate, and to complete the royal parallel he knighted the Lord Mayor before driving back by torchlight to Whitehall. Only the crowds in the street were half-hearted in their cheers. We can understand why. But we can also understand, perhaps, why Cromwell kept consistently to the policy he had adopted.

Four and a half years later he died, and his ineffective son Richard was proclaimed by the heralds as the new Lord Protector, again with all the traditional procedures. But a kingdom in disarray, that might have accepted the succession of an inadequate sovereign with royal blood, could not be held together under so new and so controversial an arrangement. The generals fell out with Richard Cromwell, the country slipped into chaos, and recovery began only when Monck marched down with his army from the Scottish border and occupied London, thereby emphasizing the essential importance of controlling the city.

The heady spirit of those days is immortally distilled in the pages of the diary Pepys was just beginning in his humble lodgings in Axe Yard, near what is now Horse Guards Parade. The coffee-houses humming with rumour, the unpaid soldiers demonstrating in the streets for 'a free Parliament and money', and then the hysterical rejoicings when Monck declared himself in favour of new elections – all are vividly caught by that observant young Londoner. 'Bow bells and all the bells in all the churches . . . a-ringing,' he wrote. 'But the common joy that was everywhere to be seen! The number of bonfires, there being fourteen between St Dunstan's and Temple Bar. And at Strand Bridge I could at one view tell 31 fires.'

That was the night of 11 February 1660. On 29 May, amid no less rejoicings, London was welcoming Charles II home from his exile in Holland.

Erra Paters Prophesy or Frost Faire 168

Roasting an Ox

Slyding in Skeats

The Posts of

Playh

The Loyall
Printing house

A Coach crossing the Ice

A Bull baiting

The Musike Booth

William
Bence

Three Pilgrims
returning from E.H.

The River of Thames

A Boate Sayling on the Ice

Old Erra Pater, or his rambling Ghost,
Prognosticating of this long strong frost,
Some Ages past. Said, y ye Ice-bound Thames
Shou'd prove a Theatre for Sports and Games,
Her Watry Green be turn'd into a Bare,
For Men a Citty seem, for Booth a Faire;

And now this Stragling Sprite is once more come
To Visit Mortalls and foretel their doom:
When Maids grow modest ye Dissenting Crew
Become all Loyal the Falsehearted true,
Then you may probably, and not til then
Expect in England such a Frost agen.

Printed for James Norris at the Kings armes without Temple Barr

The Fire – and After

Colour and gaiety returned to the city with a rush. There was a real king in Whitehall again, a witty, pleasure-loving bachelor of thirty, swift to restore the outward shows of the old order, too wily to upset people by trying to reverse the more fundamental changes that had come to stay. There were a few savage reprisals on those political leaders who had not had the foresight to die in their beds or escape abroad before the Cavaliers returned. Londoners stared, with mixed and masked feelings, at the barbarous executions of the regicides and the gloating indignities heaped on the exhumed corpse of Cromwell. But these were just grimmer spectacles, alternating with happier ceremonies and celebrations in those early months of the Restoration. Himself unaffected in life or liberty, the man in the street was free to respond to the brighter, more interesting era that seemed to be dawning.

There was promise in the air, promise however false, such as twentieth-century Londoners were twice to experience in post-war periods.

Austerity was out. In a few months Davenant and Killigrew had revived the theatre, converting two tennis-courts in Lincoln's Inn Fields until proper playhouses could be built. Soon Londoners were relishing the scandal-ous novelty of women's roles played by women. That was the end of padded boys. The reign of Nell Gwynn was at hand.

Charles struck the keynote of his Court from the first. He was determined to enjoy not merely his own again, but other men's. On 13 July, six weeks after the King's return, Pepys was sitting up to write letters in the Whitehall apartments he had not yet quitted for his future Navy Office quarters near the Tower. He was distracted by 'great doings of musique at the next house' and being a lover of 'musique' as well as incurably inquisitive, he went to the old door that led into the adjacent building and 'did stand listening a great while'. He knew that his neighbours were Roger Palmer and his beautiful wife, formerly Barbara Villiers, married only a year before. He knew that young Mrs Palmer was at that moment entertaining both the King and his brother James, and that she was 'a pretty woman that they have a fancy to, to make her husband a cuckold'. Pepys did not know that in fact, by that early date, the King had already done so. Barbara was launched on her royal progress. Two years later Roger was consoled by ennoblement as Earl of Castlemaine, and after another eight years Barbara, as a kind of redundancy payment, was created Duchess of Cleveland in her own right. She had earned her promotion by providing no less than six of the King's fourteen acknowledged bastards. Charles, ever generous with what cost him nothing, created the boys Dukes of Cleveland, Grafton and Northumberland respectively.

Opposite A broadsheet on the great frost of 1683 recalled an old prophecy that the Thames would freeze over. Of two men 'slyding in skeats', one has come to grief. Even an early form of ice-yachting can be seen.

Chiswick from the river.
Charles II was a keen
yachtsman, having acquired
the taste from the Dutch.

Whitehall was certainly an altered place. The seriousness of the Lord
Protector's Court, the decent elegance of Charles I's, the crudity of James's,
had been succeeded by a new order, in which cynical immorality was at
least carried off with style. The new king had a vitality, not entirely channelled
in one direction. He rose early, however late his nights, and tired his courtiers
with his swift walk, his love of tennis, his yachting on the river. But, though
he gave his personal attention to affairs of government, it soon flagged. More
and more, the details were delegated to committees and commissioners.
Pepys, tirelessly labouring to create an efficient administrative machine, found
it increasingly hard to get the prompt top-level decisions he required.

His diary, with its incessant mention of his journeys to and fro, from 'the
Office' in Seething Lane to wait upon the King or the Duke of York at
Whitehall, serves to emphasize the increasing division of the city into the
old and the new. Pepys lived and worked in that warren of crooked alleys
and beetling timbered houses that was soon to be swept away by the Great
Fire. He could rise from his desk and walk out into the world he had known
since childhood. He could browse among the bookshops of St Paul's
Churchyard and buy the printed play he had seen yesterday at the new theatre
in Drury Lane. He could drop into his old school, hear the boys recite, and
hobnob with the present High Master. He could take a snack in a tavern
and gossip with a rich variety of friends and acquaintances, ships' captains
and city merchants, scholarly clergymen and Fellows of the Royal Society,
who met every Wednesday afternoon at Gresham College in Bishopsgate
Street to watch scientific demonstrations and hear lectures. But when he
took boat up-river or a coach westwards along the Strand to report to his
royal masters, he entered another world.

Both Whitehall and the whole West End were changing fast. Charles,
ever short of money, and preferring human architecture to any other, did not
revive his grandfather's ambitious plans for the palace. He contented himself
with some improvements to St James's, where he and his brother had been
born. Wren was in due course commissioned to add some state apartments

Opposite This portrait of
Charles II was painted in
1670 by Sir Peter Lely for
the Hudson's Bay Company
to commemorate the grant of
the royal charter.

King Charles. II

facing the park. St James's was assigned to the Duke of York, and all his children, the future Queens Mary II and Anne and the Old Pretender, were born there too.

Charles stayed in Whitehall, and it was in the park stretching between the two palaces that he made his creative contribution. The grounds had been first laid out by Henry VIII. James I had established the aviary which gave its name to Birdcage Walk. On the far side, Pall Mall – then part of St James's Park – was so called from the French game, *paille maille*, played there just before the Civil War. It was something between croquet and golf (itself introduced by James from Scotland) and the ball had to be knocked through hoops dangling in the air. Charles II revived the game and laid out the Mall on which to play it, as being quieter than the original ground, which was accordingly cut off the park and used for building. There was no thought then of using the Mall as a processional way: the site of the future Buckingham Palace was at that date occupied by Goring (later Arlington) House and by the Mulberry Garden, planted by James I as an encouragement to the silk industry and subsequently turned into a popular pleasure resort.

St James's Park itself had degenerated with neglect. Some of the trees had been cut down for fuel in those hard winters of the Civil War blockade. In France Charles had seen the gardens designed for Louis XIV by Le Nôtre and he admired the grandiose symmetrical French style. There is no evidence that Le Nôtre, as sometimes suggested, ever came to England to supervise the work, but Charles's own gardener, John Rose, had studied under the master at Versailles, and it was in his style that St James's Park was redesigned. New trees were planted in well-ordered lines and various ponds were united to form a 'canal'. Charles was the first to throw open the park to all the public and to introduce the ducks that entertain them to this day. Here he established the first pelican in 1665, a great novelty, noted by Evelyn in his diary as 'a melancholy waterfowl brought from Astracan by the Russian Ambassador'. Earlier, Evelyn was no less impressed by the dexterity of the skaters, 'after the manner of the Hollanders', when 'the new canal' froze over in the hard December of 1662.

Outside the royal precincts development was rapid, and the latter half of the century saw the street-plan of the modern West End laid out and largely named. Charles quickly agreed to reduce the old restrictions on fresh building, and they could be ignored altogether if the developer was a favoured courtier like Henry Jermyn, that scoundrelly character so bitterly attacked by Marvell, who spoke of his 'drayman's shoulders' and his 'butcher's mien'.

Houses sprang up along Pall Mall. Nell Gwynn had one, and could jest with the King across his own park wall. St James's Fields became St James's Square and its surrounding streets, the names of which – King, Charles II, Duke of York, Cleveland, Arlington, Ormond and the rest, not forgetting Jermyn – read like a court circular. Piccadilly blossomed. Clarendon built himself a palatial mansion, later sold to the Duke of Albemarle, who gave it his own name. Noble neighbours put up Burlington House and Berkeley House.

One could wish that Aubrey had left us another volume of *Brief Lives* devoted exclusively to the characters whose names survive in the streets and

Opposite London's street-plan begins to take shape. *Top* Burlington House, Piccadilly; *bottom* St James's Square, seen from Pall Mall, with St James's Church, Piccadilly, behind.

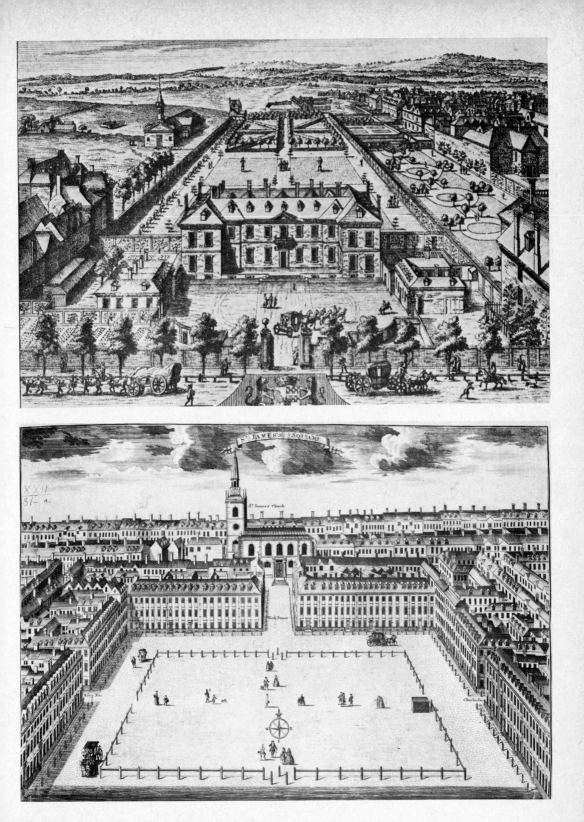

St JAMES'S SQUARE

St James's Church

York Street

A grim relic of the Plague: a handbell of the type used to warn passers-by of the approaching corpse-cart.

Token commemorating the erection of the Monument after the Great Fire, which began some seventy yards from the spot.

squares of this period, men such as Thomas Bond, Richard Frith and George Downing. The last was surprisingly a native of Massachusetts and one of the earliest Harvard graduates. In New England he was a byword for treachery and London came to know him as a master of espionage and intrigue. He was an expert political fixer. Marvell dubbed him 'the house-bell to call the courtiers to vote'. The street which commemorates him could scarcely be more appropriate. Only an obscure cul-de-sac off Great Ormond Street, Barbon Close, recalls Dr Nicholas Barbon, son of 'Praise-God Barebones', as unscrupulous a speculator as Jermyn but one whose arrogance did not recommend him to the King. Barbon's contribution to the new London included developments in Soho, the whole area between the Strand and the river, and Red Lion Fields. He was a buccaneer in his methods, turning out with two hundred workmen to intimidate protesters, and threatening to mobilize a thousand more.

Before this, however, the Great Fire of 1666 had produced a dramatic transformation of the older city to the east.

It was a stunning catastrophe, coming a year after the last outbreak of plague, but it was one reason why that outbreak *was* the last. The pestilence killed tens of thousands, sent the Court scurrying to safety at Oxford, and caused the various government departments to disperse into the country. The fire, starting slowly and giving ample warning as it spread, seems to have caused very few deaths (and some of those were murders, doubtless in the course of looting) but it laid waste the old crowded, insanitary city from the Tower to Temple Bar. The flames spread north as far as London Wall. They seized one end of London Bridge but could not cross to Southwark. Buckets and fire-hooks were useless against such a blaze. The King and his brother brought men from the dockyards to demolish houses with gunpowder and to establish fire-breaks, but it was chiefly the slackening of the east wind that finally halted the conflagration.

The smouldering ruins covered some 436 acres, four-fifths of the old city. St Paul's, Guildhall, the Royal Exchange, many of the livery halls and other public buildings were gone or gutted, together with over eighty parish churches and thirteen thousand dwellings. These last, on average, had housed more people than the equivalent number would have done today, what with the large families and their servants, the journeymen and apprentices. The total left homeless has been variously estimated between one and two hundred thousand. While some of the more prosperous had managed to load their chattels into wagons or barges, and escape to friends or their own retreats in the country, the vast majority had nowhere to go but Moorfields or Hampstead Heath, where the government improvised tents and hutted camps and organized such disaster relief as was then feasible.

The famous resilience of the Londoners was never more conspicuous than in those September days. Most families had still been mourning the bereavements of the plague. It would have been understandable if this second calamity had stunned them into hopelessness. Yet as early as 10 September – the fire had burned until the 6th – Henry Oldenburg was writing to Robert Boyle at Oxford: 'The citizens, instead of complaining, discoursed almost of nothing but of a survey for rebuilding the city with bricks and large streets.'

The Fire of London was a
stunning catastrophe, but
also a swift and radical
sterilization of a plague-spot.
Top The fire at its height:
this painting shows the glare
of the flames reflected from
the Tower, which escaped.
Centre The fire engines of that
time were of little use; houses
were blown up to make fire-
breaks. *Bottom* The aftermath.
This detail from a panorama
by Hollar is dominated by
the roofless shell of St Paul's.

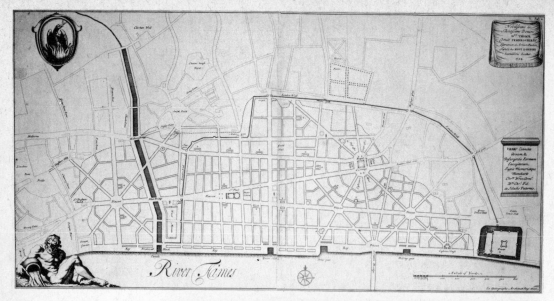

Wren's plan for a new London was a visionary but impractical affair of piazzas and broad, straight boulevards, with twin foci at St Paul's (left) and the Royal Exchange. It was produced only five days after the Fire had ended.

Sir Christopher Wren. Though his over-all plan was rejected, his designs set the style of the rebuilt city.

After the fire, the frost. In 1677 the Thames was frozen from bank to bank. Such scenes recurred until the old bridge of many arches was replaced in 1831.

Seldom can experts and officials have sprung so smartly to answer a popular demand. That same day Evelyn recorded in his diary: 'I went again to the ruins; for it was now no longer a city.' Then he set to work, and on the 13th could make this entry: 'I presented his Majesty with a survey of the ruins and a plot for a new City, with a discourse on it.' Wren, however, had produced his rival scheme two days earlier. Other plans poured in – from the versatile inventor, Robert Hooke, from Sir William Petty, statistician, political economist and late surveyor-general in Ireland, from the city's own surveyor, Peter Mills, striving to hold his own against all these eminent Fellows of the Royal Society, and from other ingenious individuals confident that they had the perfect answer to the problem.

Most of these schemes were visually splendid, more aesthetic than practical. It is easy to lament the broad straight streets and riverside embankments, the vistas and piazzas and other noble features that were destined to remain for ever on paper – 'unhappily defeated by faction', as the subsequently printed copy of Wren's plan declared – but it is harder to see how they could have been realized in the circumstances of the time. Confronted with such a bewildering choice of New Jerusalems, Charles might well have felt his brain boiling under his wig. Sensibly, he handed over the decision to a committee of six, three to be chosen by the city. His own nominees were Wren, Roger Pratt, the architect, and Hugh May, Paymaster of the Works. All had travelled widely abroad.

Theirs was a daunting commission. To rehouse the homeless was the obvious priority: winter was approaching, and there were some notably hard winters in that period, with more than one Frost Fair held on a Thames frozen from bank to bank. But in pursuit of this object they had to reconcile two frequently incompatible considerations – the prevention of future fires and epidemics by a more spacious layout and the preservation of existing freehold rights by innumerable owners, large and small. The marvel is not

Montague House in Great Russell Street, one of the many palatial new mansions put up in the years after the Great Fire. In 1759 it became the British Museum, being demolished in 1852 when the present larger buildings were being developed on the site.

that London – in theory – missed a great opportunity, but that agreement on a measure of planning was possible at all, and that reconstruction went forward as fast as it did.

Some things at least could be settled with authority. Parliament could lay down regulations about building materials, the number of storeys permitted in various streets, and the prohibition of projecting signs, water-spouts and other obstructions. Parishes could be merged to accord with the needs of the period, so that, although eighty-seven churches had been burnt, only fifty-five new ones were built. Wren had the general supervision of these, providing the plans, but designed only a few in detail himself, leaving the rest to the craftsmen on the job. The church-building did not start in earnest until 1670, and only in 1675 could he begin on his masterpiece, the new St Paul's.

All this had to be paid for – and at a time when England had not funds to keep her fleet at sea, and the Dutch were free to sail up to the Medway. as they did the following year, and burn the English warships at their anchorage. Yet somehow London rose again. The churches were paid for by a tax on coal, the city and its livery companies rebuilt their own properties, but the individual businessman and householder had to meet his costs without help from anyone. There were no fire insurance companies before 1680, and if there had been they would surely have been bankrupt.

The Great Fire did not merely change the outward face of the city, making it as shining new as the West End: it altered its human geography too. Some people never came back, or, if they returned to trade, preferred to make new homes in the suburbs. In their places, and in far greater numbers than those who left, came an influx of craftsmen and labourers from every part of the country, and even from abroad. The amount of reconstruction to be done made London a kind of Klondike for every branch of the building industry. As the years passed, too, quite other factors caused further immigration from abroad. The revocation of the Edict of Nantes in 1685 brought a wave of French Protestants, who settled mainly in the East End and especially in Spitalfields, where they established the silk industry.

Opposite Wren's St Paul's still dominates the city skyline, as he intended it to do.

The most marked foreign influence on London, however, throughout this period was undoubtedly Dutch. From Pepys's visit in 1660, when he helped to bring home the King and was impressed by The Hague, 'a most neat place in all respects', until fifty years later, when Marlborough House was built of bricks carried as ballast in the empty vessels returning from Holland after supplying the Duke's armies there, the Dutch contribution whether in human or material terms, technical processes or commercial methods, was incalculable. Whether as commercial rivals and enemies in war, or later as allies under William III's leadership, the English and the Dutch were inextricably involved with each other. All England felt the Dutch influence, but London more than anywhere. Amsterdam was the centre of international trade. The establishment of the Harwich packet service in 1687 – a year before William came over, it may be noted – meant that a London businessman could correspond more easily with a customer in Amsterdam than with one in the more distant English towns.

This was the age when the Dutch were pre-eminent not only in art but in a dozen other fields where there was scope for progress and brilliant innovation. Charles, James and their courtiers might admire the France of Louis. Londoners looked to Holland with the kind of respect (mixed with other emotions) that their descendants would later accord to America. In 1665, when the plague had brought normal business to a standstill, Sir Josiah Child set down his *Brief Observations concerning Trade and the Interest of Money*, in which seminal work he declared that

the prodigious increase of the Netherlands in their domestic and foreign trade, riches and multitude of shipping, is the envy of the present, and may be the wonder of all future generations: and yet the means whereby they have thus advanced themselves are sufficiently obvious, and in a great measure imitable by most other nations, but more easily by us. . . .

Opposite In College Hill, near the Mansion House, this building, rebuilt after the fire, is now an office and a wine-bar.

Above Lambeth Delft-ware slab showing the arms of the Apothecaries' Company. *Below* The Horse Ferry at Lambeth (about 1700) was licensed by the Archbishop of Canterbury, but the nude bathers presumably were not.

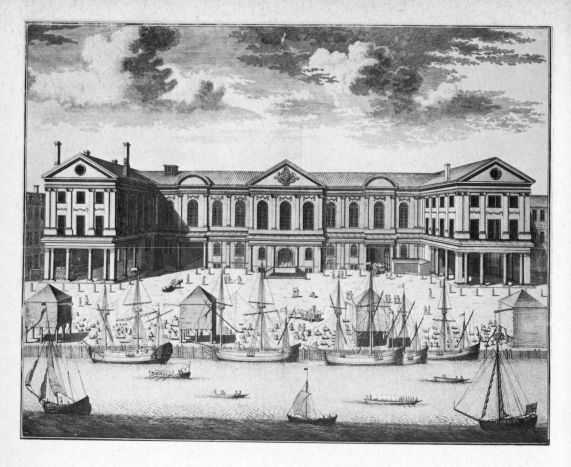

Built in 1669–74, the Old Customs House was designed by Wren. It was burned down in the early eighteenth century and is now known only from engravings, no plans having survived.

Eight years later, another famous Londoner, Sir William Temple, wrote his more general *Observations on the United Provinces of the Netherlands*, which was widely read and discussed. He emphasized the low interest rates in Holland, the plentiful capital lying 'ready for all projects, by which gain may be expected'. He praised the efficiency of Dutch business methods and in particular their banks. England had as yet no proper banks, and financial transactions still depended on the goldsmiths – who had suffered badly in the crisis of 1672, the year before Temple's book came out.

Child and Temple were not alone in advising their fellow-citizens to cast their eyes across the North Sea. There was a spate of books and pamphlets on Holland, as well as translations from the Dutch.

Not least admired was the Dutch success in opening up trade in remote continents. The English had long ago followed them to the East Indies. Since the acquisition of Bombay as part of the dowry that came with Charles's Portuguese bride, the East India Company had been slowly establishing itself on the Indian mainland, though unable to displace the Dutch in the islands. The London merchants were involved in other overseas ventures. The Hudson's Bay Company was founded in 1670 with Prince Rupert as first governor, and the Royal Africa Company two years later, dealing mainly in slaves and with the Duke of York at its head. The ill-fated South Sea

Company was formed much later, in 1710, to exploit the Pacific. On the whole, despite some slow starts and sensational failures, British trade was emerging vigorously from the doldrums, political and economic, of the earlier part of the century.

Relations between the Crown and the City remained uneasy, as they always had been under the Stuart kings. There was antipathy in almost all respects. The typical London merchant was a Protestant individualist, a Whig, a cultivator of the domestic virtues. To him the Court was a hotbed of immorality, veiled or even open Catholicism, and Frenchified fashions, and he might have found it hard to say which he thought the worst. Normally the London mob could be depended upon to turn out in a crisis and howl down the King's Tory supporters, and in his later years, desperately trying to get a Parliament he could control, Charles was forced to summon it to Oxford instead of Westminster. Similarly, in his efforts to get subservient M.P.s elected, he treated London as he did many of the smaller towns: since, under the restricted franchise, M.P.s were virtually chosen by the local councillors in each place, he revoked their charters. London's was forfeited like many another and replaced with one that put the control of the Common Council in the hands of the King. Such dictatorial actions might make possible the controversial succession of Catholic James to the throne, but they also made feasible the Glorious Revolution of 1688.

James's reign was short but full of drama. He tried to overawe his capital by building up a large army on Hounslow Heath. He clapped the famous 'Seven Bishops' into the Tower for seditious libel, but no amount of rigging could secure a conviction. London went mad with joy when the bishops were acquitted, and even the troops at Hounslow cheered. The most significant surviving reminder of James is the weathercock on the Banqueting House in Whitehall, set up by the apprehensive monarch in 1686 so that he could watch for the 'Protestant wind', which sure enough brought William's expeditionary force to dethrone him two years later.

Naturally, the Dutch influence was stronger than ever after that. Dutch businessmen, and Jews from Holland, took up permanent residence in London. One community grew up round Austin Friars, the old monastic building that Edward VI had assigned to Protestant refugees in general. It now acquired its more specific label, the Dutch Church. The Jews had a synagogue in Creechurch Lane, which they removed in 1701 to the neighbouring Heneage Lane. All that area, round Bevis Marks, became the focus of the Jewish community.

The initiative for founding the Bank of England is usually attributed to a Scot, William Paterson, a picturesque and widely travelled character, said to have been at various times both a preacher and a buccaneer, who had settled in London and been enrolled in the Merchant Taylors Company. But, though he was a director of the Bank when it was established in 1694, he quickly dropped out, and the main inspiration was Dutch. Indeed, 'Dutch finance' was a favourite Tory phrase in deriding it. Not only was the model provided by Amsterdam, but Dutchmen put their money into the new British institution, just as they bought the British stocks quoted on their own Bourse.

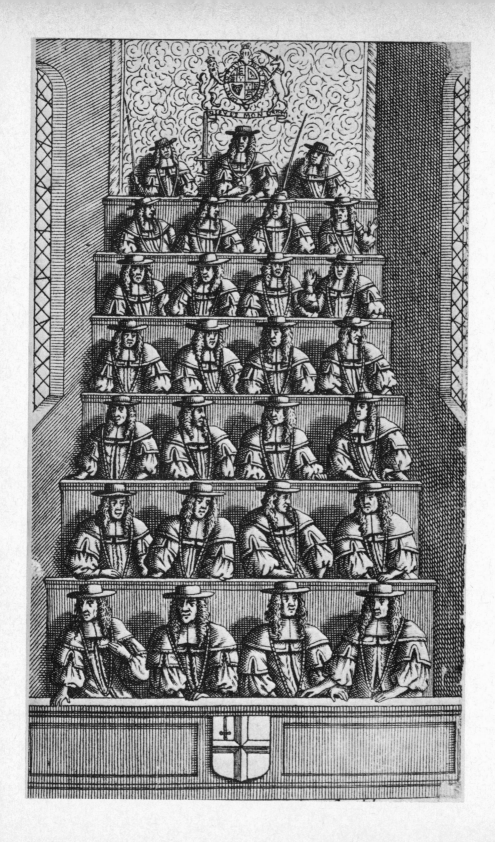

One by one London's great financial institutions were coming into existence. Lloyd's had evolved as an exchange of shipping news – the first field in which insurance was arranged – when Edward Lloyd's coffee-house opened in Great Tower Street in James's reign, and moved to Lombard Street in 1691. Similarly, as London advanced into the eighteenth century, the Virginia and Baltic Coffee House gave birth to the Baltic Exchange and the Jerusalem Coffee House became the venue of the Shipping Exchange, two bodies that amalgamated in 1899.

In 1710, with the last stone of St Paul's laid in place, one could say that the new London of Wren was complete. The same date saw another kind of new London firmly established, displaying in outline at least the world centre of finance and commerce that was to grow throughout the eighteenth and nineteenth centuries.

Opposite The Lord Mayor and aldermen: often at loggerheads with an increasingly high-handed King.

Below Two wooden moulds for gingerbread give an unusual and attractive view of Stuart fashions.

The Georgian Century

'By the Revolution we got a shabby family to reign over us,' noted Boswell in 1763, and his comment applies with special force to the earlier Hanoverian period.

William III may have been an unattractive foreigner, with scant interest in London, but he was politically welcome, brought a needed breath of change, and had a lovable if unremarkable English queen. George I, equally un-attractive and foreign, arrived from Hanover with no such compensating assets. His succession to Anne aroused about as much enthusiasm as James I's to Elizabeth. He was simply the nearest royal relative with a Protestant qualification.

Almost symbolically, he was fog-bound in the Thames on arrival and misunderstandings began from the moment when, well behind schedule, he stepped ashore in the darkness at Greenwich. His son had landed first, been mistaken for him, and been accorded the honours intended for the sovereign. Explanations were not easy. George I knew no English and relied mainly on French, which he spoke badly, as did most of his new courtiers. With his Prime Minister, Walpole, he normally communicated, or failed to communi-cate, in Latin. The English pronounced this language in a manner all their own, which others, even Scots like Boswell, found hard to follow.

After two nights at Greenwich George and his son drove through deco-rated streets and dutifully cheering crowds to St James's Palace, which had once more become the official seat of the Court since the burning down of Whitehall in 1698 through the carelessness of a Dutch laundress. William had never liked either palace. The smoke of Westminster had irritated his asthma, and in his first year he had bought Nottingham House from the earl of that name, renamed it Kensington Palace, and made it the chief royal residence in London, which it remained until the death of George II, whose successor bought Buckingham House.

At St James's the first Hanoverian sovereign kept up the most austere establishment. He slept and took his meals in the same room, and used only one other, in which he received his ministers. His privacy was guarded by two incongruous Pages of the Backstairs, Mahomet and Mustapha, Turks taken prisoner in his youthful campaigns of long ago.

There was no queen. George had divorced his unfaithful wife and im-prisoned her for life in a German castle. At first her social duties in London were discharged by his son's wife, Caroline, now Princess of Wales, but it was not long before sovereign and heir fell out. The future George II was expelled from St James's and excluded from Court. He and his Princess

Opposite Northumberland House, Charing Cross, looking west. James Boswell, attending a 'magnificent rout' there in 1763, was reminded of the splendours of Holyroodhouse. Sole survivor of this great town house is the lion over the entrance, which is now at Syon House, Brentford.

removed to Leicester House and identified themselves with the Tory opposition, a pattern of family discord that was to be repeated by their own son, Frederick, and to recur often in later generations.

The most prominent ladies at George I's Court were two Germans, generally assumed in London to be his mistresses, though one, Fräulein von Kielmannsegge, was in fact his illegitimate half-sister. He gave her the title of Countess of Darlington, but she was of such massive proportions that the disrespectful Londoners nicknamed her 'the Elephant and Castle', while the taller and thinner Fräulein von Schulenberg, though ennobled as Duchess of Kendal, was more popularly known as 'the Maypole'.

Both George I and George II preferred Hanover to England, and their influence on London was mainly negative. The linguistic barrier isolated them. At all levels, from Cabinet and Parliament downwards, life went on without them. Their chief positive contribution can be seen at Kensington. Wren and Hawksmoor had already improved the palace for William and then for Anne. Kent was commissioned to make further internal alterations for George I, who also planned the Broad Walk and the Round Pond, but it was his daughter-in-law who, as Queen Caroline, proceeded with his scheme and in 1733 created the Serpentine by damming the waters of the little Westbourne river. Until this time there was still deer-hunting in Hyde Park, which Henry VIII had taken from Westminster Abbey and turned into a hunting ground. It had also been a centre of fashion since Charles I, who first laid out the Ring as a promenade for the coaches of the quality, but the place had been equally frequented by footpads and it was only in Georgian times that it began to become even relatively safe and respectable.

Kensington Palace, bought from the Earl of Nottingham by William III. The country air of Kensington suited the King's asthma better than the smoke of Westminster.

The isolation of the sovereign ceased with the accession in 1760 of Caroline's twenty-two-year-old grandson, George III, the first English-born and English-speaking Hanoverian king. If this young man could have had his

The Mansion House, official residence of the Lord Mayor, was built in 1739–53.

own way, he would have looked no further than Kensington for a wife, for, as he took his regular morning ride, he used to see Lady Sarah Lennox elegantly haymaking on the lawns of Holland House and fell passionately in love with her. But, though a newly proclaimed king, he could not please himself in this, and within the year he was dutifully marrying Charlotte Sophia of Mecklenburg-Strelitz. Lady Sarah, by cruel irony, was one of the bridesmaids. The royal marriage turned out happily enough, but it could only prolong the German atmosphere of the Court.

It was in the following year that James Boswell arrived in the capital, took lodgings in Downing Street, and opened that private journal which, for the picture it gives of contemporary society, compares with Pepys's diary of just a century earlier. Scots were now so plentiful in London – one of them, Lord Bute, was even Prime Minister – that Boswell, alternately proud of and apologetic for his nationality, had to make constant efforts to avoid the exclusive company of his fellow-countrymen.

One January morning, with two other young men, he kept a resolution to walk from one end of London to the other. They started from Hyde Park Corner at ten, breakfasted at the Somerset Coffee House in the Strand, and continued through the City to London Bridge, 'whence we viewed with a pleasing horror the rude and terrible appearance of the river, partly froze up, partly covered with enormous shoals of floating ice which often crashed against each other.' A fire in 1758 had caused the removal of the last houses from the bridge, which was still under repair. Fortunately, it was no longer the sole road-crossing of the Thames. The first Westminster Bridge (later to inspire Wordsworth's famous sonnet) had been completed in 1750 by a

Swiss engineer, Charles Labelye, and a Scots acquaintance of Boswell's, Robert Mylne, was even then building one at Blackfriars.

That winter walk prompted Boswell to quote the *Spectator*, that 'one end of London is like a different country from the other in look and in manners'. His *London Journal* ranges widely through both.

The West End, where his social ambitions centred, was still growing and changing. Some noble mansions of an earlier period remained. He attended a 'magnificent rout' at Northumberland House, where the size and adorn-ment of the 'prodigious' gallery reminded him of Holyrood. Most of the aristocracy, however, were rebuilding their old town houses or commissioning new ones. Under the first two Georges the fashionable architect had been William Kent, the Earl of Burlington's Yorkshire protégé. He had helped to redesign his patron's Piccadilly home in 1719. Among many other commissions he had built Devonshire House for the third Duke, cultivating an unpretentious simplicity which caused one critic to compare the building to an East India Company warehouse. There was no dull uniformity in the new Georgian town that was springing up. Thomas Archer, who built Harcourt House for Lord Bingley in the 1720s, was an enthusiast for the baroque. *His* design was attacked as being more 'like a convent than the residence of a man of quality'. And by the time Boswell reached London the Gothic revival was beginning. Its pioneer, the gifted amateur Sanderson Miller, had just built a house in Arlington Street, which, with its gatehouse and forecourt, earned the nickname of 'Pomfret Castle'.

Many other notable houses were either newly built or in process of building at this date. Chesterfield House, designed for the famous earl of that name by

Scene in a coffee-house, about 1700. Coffee-houses came into their own in the eighteenth century, as meeting-places for business, discussion or conversation. Lloyd's and other great mercantile institutions evolved from such rendezvous.

Devonshire House, built by William Kent for the 3rd Duke; its classically simple Georgian design was likened by a contemporary critic to a warehouse. It was demolished by developers in 1924.

the royal surveyor, Isaac Ware, had been completed in 1752. So had Norfolk House in St James's Square. The Duke's earlier house on that site had been leased to Frederick, Prince of Wales, and had in fact been the birthplace of George III. A later house, built in 1939, was to provide Eisenhower with a headquarters in the second World War.

When Boswell took up his residence in Downing Street, Kent had been dead for fourteen years, but the young Scot, then persistently canvassing for an army commission, had only to stroll round the corner to the Horse Guards to see the last example of his work. A few yards further on, appropriately, rose the elegant stone screen of the Admiralty designed in 1759 by Robert Adam, the architect who more than any other was to fill Kent's place for the second half of the century.

Adam was not long returned from those Italian and Dalmatian travels that so profoundly influenced him. In 1761 he had been appointed architect of the royal works jointly with his fellow Scot, Sir William Chambers, best known for his Somerset House and the pagoda and orangery at Kew. Adam, with his brothers, created much of the West End. In 1762 he was building Lansdowne House in Berkeley Square, originally for Lord Bute. The Adelphi followed, inspired by the remains of Diocletian's palace at Split. He built Apsley House, and many more, singly or in terraces, in Mansfield Street, St James's Square, Portman Square and Fitzroy Square.

Here was the world of rank and fashion in which Boswell sought advancement, but, to do him justice, his interests were by no means confined to it, and when (his landlord complaining too brusquely after a noisy party) he was forced to quit Downing Street for 'genteel . . . chambers in that calm retreat', the Inner Temple, he found the mode of living there 'the most agreeable in the world for a single man'. He enjoyed watching the Guards drill before the palace but he was as ready to go – once at all events – to see a man hanged at Tyburn, when he 'was most terribly shocked and thrown into a very deep melancholy'. He had all Pepys's curiosity, though without Pepys's work to do. His journal takes us into the House of Lords to hear George III's speech from the throne, into the Commons to listen to Henry Fox and the

Top The south front of
Robert Adam's Adelphi,
inspired by his visit to
Diocletian's palace at Split.

Above The Thames at
Mortlake in 1753.

elder Pitt, and into the court of Sir John Fielding, the blind Bow Street
magistrate who so ably continued his brother Henry's battle against the
criminal gangs then infesting London. With Boswell we climb to the top of
the Monument or the roof of St Paul's to survey the city spread below, walk
out to Islington to take tea with Goldsmith or to Kensington to 'stroll through
the delightful Gardens', dine at the Beefsteak Club in Covent Garden, sup
with Johnson at the Turk's Head in the Strand, and pay a regular Saturday
visit to Child's Coffee House in St Paul's Churchyard, 'quite a place to
my mind; dusky, comfortable and warm, with a society of citizens and phy-
sicians who talk politics very fully and are very sagacious and sometimes
jocular.'

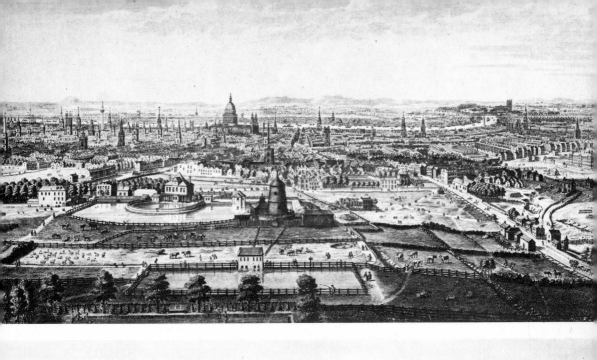

Top View from the Bowling Green, Islington, southwards to St Paul's. Myddleton's Clerkenwell reservoir is seen, left of centre.

Above Covent Garden, with the first Opera House, opened in 1732. *Left* Courtyard of the Tabard Inn, Southwark, starting-point of Chaucer's Canterbury pilgrims.

Boswell's evenings were no less varied. He could see Garrick's Lear at Drury Lane, hear Arne's *Artaxerxes* at Covent Garden, and 'laugh much' at Tate Wilkinson, 'a most admirable mimic', at Foote's Little Theatre in the Haymarket. For sixpence he could attend the Robin Hood Society at the tavern of that name in Butcher Row near the Temple – a debating society frequented not by lawyers but by artisans and tradesmen, an interesting indica/tion of the political consciousness already manifesting itself among those who still had no say in the nation's government. In a less serious mood he could drive in a friend's coach to one of the pleasure/gardens, either Vauxhall, 'which was quite delicious', since a quarrel between a gentleman and a waiter almost caused a riot, or Ranelagh, 'an entertainment quite peculiar to London', where 'the noble Rotunda all surrounded with boxes to sit in and such a profusion of well/dressed people walking round is very fine.'

Some of his diversions were more private. 'I am surrounded', he noted after his first few weeks in the city, 'with numbers of free/hearted ladies of all kinds: from the splendid Madam at fifty guineas a night, down to the civil nymph with white/thread stockings who tramps along the Strand and will resign her engaging person to your honour for a pint of wine and a shilling.' Sometimes, indeed, his furtive fumblings in the park cost him only sixpence. Once, having 'picked up a strong, jolly young damsel' in the Haymarket, he 'conducted her to Westminster Bridge, and . . . did . . . engage her upon this noble edifice. The whim of doing it there with the Thames rolling below us amused me very much.' Georgian London certainly comes to life in *Boswell's Journal*.

That, of course, is only incidental. He was writing for himself and for a single distant friend, and lengthy descriptions formed no part of his plan. For these we have to turn to the more deliberately informative accounts of other strangers in the city, especially visitors from the Continent.

The most critical was perhaps the French lawyer, Peter John Grosley, who was in London a few years after Boswell was writing. He was scathing about the treatment of the Thames. 'All possible measures have been taken to conceal the prospect of this fine river. . . . The banks are occupied by tanners, dyers and other manufacturers. . . . The streets where these manu/factures are carried on are the dirtiest in the city, and the bridges have no prospect of the river except through a balustrade of stone.' He remarked on the Londoners' propensity to commit suicide in the Thames, and attributed it to fog and an excessive diet of beef and beer. A German historian, J. W. von Archenholtz, on the other hand, praised the new bridges at Westminster and Blackfriars as 'exceedingly well/paved and adorned with balustrades of stone', though he too commented on the numerous suicides and actually witnessed one.

Grosley complained of the fog, the cost of living, the pickpockets, the inadequacy of the elderly watchmen, and the fury of a London mob, a notorious phenomenon of that period. Luckily he was not there in 1780 when the unbalanced aristocrat, Lord George Gordon, so whipped up anti/Catholic feeling that a wild rabble terrorized the capital for a fortnight. Grosley found the streets rough and dirty, but other foreign visitors paint a more favourable picture. The Swiss physicist and Alpine pioneer, de

A London courtesan. Boswell was a connoisseur of such 'civil nymphs' and 'free/hearted ladies'.

Bathing in the Fleet river: an illustration from Pope's *Dunciad*.

Saussure, admired the raised pavements, the mud-carts and water-carts, and the street-lighting: each house, he said, had a lamp burning outside all night, and great mansions had as many as four. Archenholtz declared that 'in Oxford Road alone there are more lamps than in all the city of Paris.' Grosley seems to have conceded the attractions of this thoroughfare, but only to prophesy that 'the shops of Oxford Street will disappear as the houses are sought after for private dwellings by the rich. Soon will the great city extend

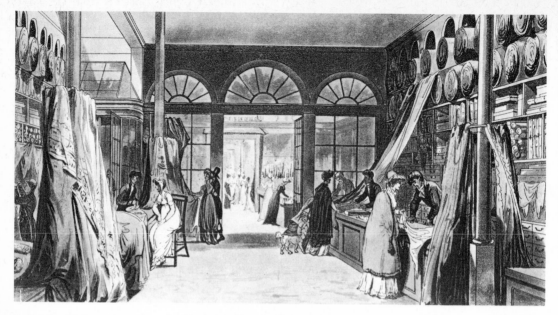

A fashionable linen draper's in Pall Mall, about 1800.

itself to Marylebone, which is not more than a quarter of a league distant. At present it is a village, principally of taverns inhabited by French refugees.'

Oxford Street was still a lively shopping street, despite Grosley's forecast, when Sophie von la Roche saw it twenty years later in 1786.

We strolled up and down lovely Oxford Street this evening [she wrote], for some goods look more attractive by artificial light. Just imagine a street taking half an hour to cover from end to end, with double rows of brightly shining lamps, in the middle of which stands an equally long row of beautifully lacquered coaches, and on either side of these there is room for two coaches to pass one another; and the pavement, inlaid with flagstones, can stand six people deep and allows one to gaze at the splendidly lit shop-fronts in comfort. Behind great glass windows absolutely everything one can think of is neatly, attractively displayed.

A more precise idea of what the shops contained may be deduced from a description of Fleet Street in 1774 as seen by Georg Christoph Lichtenberg from Göttingen:

On both sides are tall houses with plate-glass windows, the lower floors consisting of shops and seeming to be made entirely of glass. Many thousands of candles light up silverware, engravings, books, clocks, glass, pewter, paintings, women's finery, modish and otherwise, gold, precious stones, steelwork, and endless coffee-rooms and lottery offices. The street looks as if it were illuminated for some festivity. The apothecaries and druggists display glasses filled with gay-coloured spirits, purple, yellow, verdigris-green or azure. . . . The confectioners dazzle your eyes with their candelabra and tickle your noses with their wares . . . festoons of Spanish grapes alternating with pineapples, and pyramids of apples and oranges, among which hover attendant white-armed nymphs with silk caps and little silk trains.

The traffic was considerable, 'chaises, carriages and drays in an unending stream', and the noise can hardly have been less than it is today, with 'the chimes from church towers, the bells of the postmen, the organs, fiddles,

Opposite The other end of the social scale: old clothes man.

hurdy-gurdies and tambourines of mountebanks, and the cries of those who sell hot and cold viands at the street-corners'. He noted also the quieter but equally plentiful whores and pickpockets.

Away from the shopping streets, Sophie von la Roche admired the new residential developments and found one feature particularly novel: 'An iron railing, erected some paces from the house, runs up to the front doors dividing the road from the basement, which not only contains the cellar but also kitchen, bakehouse and servants' quarters.' De Saussure similarly commented: 'A sort of moat, five or six feet in width and eight or nine deep, is dug in front of all the houses and is called "the area". The moat is edged with an iron railing.' 'Well-kept houses' of this type were washed twice a week from top to bottom, he wrote, and 'every morning most kitchens, staircases and entrances are scrubbed. All furniture, and especially all kitchen utensils, are kept with the greatest cleanliness.'

Sophie enjoyed a visit to Sadler's Wells, which had been a place of popular resort with Londoners since a Mr Sadler discovered the medicinal spring in 1684 and had begun its long theatrical tradition by building the Musick House. This wooden erection had been replaced in 1765 by a stone theatre, built in seven weeks. It offered a variety of attractions ranging from performing dogs and the infant Grimaldi to Shakespeare and (later on) stupendous aquatic spectacles in which, to quote Miss Phyllis Hartnoll, 'naval battles took place, heroines were rescued by heroes, and children by Newfoundland dogs.' Sophie's contemporary description, however, is more concerned with the general surroundings of the theatre. 'This district is very lovely,' she wrote,

with large meadows alive with herds of excellent cows, lakes with trees in front of the house itself, numerous avenues with delightful tables and benches for visitors, under trees hung with tiny lamps. In the open temple lower-class lasses, sailors and other young people were dancing. We were astonished at the handsome building and illumination of the hall.

Another observer, C.P. Moritz, praised the more scholarly attractions of the city. The British Museum, first institution of its kind in the world, had been opened in 1759 in Montague House, the late-seventeenth-century mansion which then occupied the site and still had farmlands stretching away behind it to the north. Boswell had confessed himself 'amused' by its 'numerous curiosities'. The less dilettante Moritz, who was a professor of archaeology at Berlin, wrote of the 'stupendous treasures' in a 'vast suite of rooms'. He could have spent years in pleasant contemplation, but serious study would have required a lifetime. Moritz was not so studious that he could not enjoy evenings out at Vauxhall and Ranelagh. The latter, though considered more select, proved cheaper. The half-crown admission charge included refreshments, whereas a very modest supper at Vauxhall cost 'at least half a guinea'. The relaxed atmosphere of the House of Commons shocked him. The M.P.s sprawled and even stretched out on the benches. 'Some crack nuts,' he told his readers, 'others eat oranges or whatever else is in season.'

Few of these visitors give more than incidental glimpses of the poverty which often lay behind the elegant façade. No one today can fail to be appalled by the squalor, suffering and inhumanity of the period, but it is fair to remember that conditions, compared not with those of our own period but with those of some other European capitals at the time and even those of some other English towns, were very tolerable for a large part of the population. Voltaire, arriving from the poverty of France in 1726, gained his first impressions of England at Greenwich Fair, where the working lads and servant-girls in their holiday clothes looked to him like 'people of fashion'. Some were on hired mounts. He was struck by 'the skill with which the young women managed their horses and . . . with the freshness and beauty of their complexions, the neatness of their dress and the graceful vivacity of their movements.' Later in the century, as the Industrial Revolution developed and cast its blight on the Midlands and North of England, London escaped the worst horrors. Sweated labour there was, exploitation of women and children (especially the orphan apprentices), crowded working conditions and slum housing, but there were neither coal-mines nor 'satanic mills'. London had countless manufactures but it did not depend solely upon them, nor were they all unpleasant or ill-paid. Commerce, shipping, banking, insurance, public administration, retail trade, services and entertainment then as later offered the working Londoner a wider choice of jobs than he could have found anywhere else.

Boy chimney-sweep. The exploitation of these children horrified even the hard-bitten Londoners of the eighteenth century.

Many called for high degrees of craftsmanship. One has only to think of the cabinetmakers working for Chippendale's famous shop in St Martin's Lane or for Hepplewhite's in Cripplegate, the specialized watchmakers in the garrets of Clerkenwell, the Lambeth glassworkers, the mirror-makers in the Duke of Buckingham's little factory at Vauxhall, the silversmiths employed by Paul de Lamerie, Anthony Nelme and Benjamin Pyne, and John Jackson's pioneering wallpaper transfer printers at Battersea. And there was another kind of printer, without whom Johnson's *Dictionary*, Wilkes's *North Briton*, *The Times* (from 1785) and *The Observer* (from 1791) could never have reached the eighteenth-century reader. There were the workers in china, too, producing the famous Bow figures for Thomas Frye and Edward Heylyn, or the exquisite pieces for William Sprimont at Chelsea, in mazarin blue, apple green, claret and turquoise. Hoop Alley, off Shoe Lane, was where the sign-painters congregated: this craft was in continual demand and its outstanding practitioners were artists, expecting to be paid accordingly. So too with the carvers and painters of sedan chairs and coaches, who, as a contemporary writer pointed out, must 'be pretty expert in representing naked boys, festoons of fruit, flowers and other ornaments'. William Kent began as an apprentice to a coach-painter.

At the opposite end of the scale were the hapless boy chimney-sweeps, the women cinder-sifters, the rag-pickers and the ubiquitous street vendors, whose activities too often blurred into beggary and petty crime. Between these economic extremes stretched an immense variety of employment. There were the clerks, warehousemen and countless others employed by wealthy merchants such as William Beckford, Lord Mayor in the year of Boswell's first sojourn. There were, in contrast, the Hammersmith fishermen who eked out a declining yet still independent livelihood on the waters flowing past their homes, owning their own boats and selling their catches through Billingsgate.

Fishwife at Billingsgate, a fish market since Saxon times.

There was a good deal of seasonal Irish labour. The Irishmen came over each summer to cut the hay on the dairy farms encircling London. The poverty of their own country tempted them to come too early and to stay on after the haymaking, so that they and their families swelled the hordes of beggars, hawkers and casual workers.

Then, as now, a high proportion of wives had to supplement their husbands' earnings. The Old Bailey records – listing witnesses as well as defendants – are revealing. A hackney coachman's wife is a washerwoman, a chairman is married to a milk-seller, a watchman's wife sells cakes and gingerbread. Another milk-seller falls out with her shoemaker husband, who throws one of her pails at her with fatal results but is acquitted. Less fortunate is the waterman, owner of two wherries, who is found guilty of murdering *his* wife, landlady of a public house. A carpenter's wife runs a shop, and a peruke-maker is not unsuitably matched with a milliner. More surprisingly, the wives of some professional men engage in business. An attorney's wife keeps the Kensington Coffee House, and a surgeon's has a poulterer's shop.

Apart from all these married women there were, as there always had been, widows such as Hester Bateman, the silversmith, and others carrying on the businesses of dead husbands or fathers.

For the working population the standard of life seems to have been as varied as the type of occupation. The century produced its crop of strikes, pathetic petitions, disturbing public inquiries, and heart-breaking individual cases. There were periods of high prices and acute distress, notably during the slump in foreign trade from 1763 to 1773 and again in 1792. It was possible to starve to death in eighteenth-century London, but it was equally possible to live reasonably well and get great enjoyment from life. The evidence is unanswerable that countless humble and not so humble, hard-working and not so hard-working people did.

It is equally certain that for Londoners the second half of the century showed a marked improvement on the first. Statistics and the opinion of contemporary sociologists are united on that, and the reason can be expressed in the monosyllable, 'gin', which had such a catastrophic effect on London life from about 1720 until 1751, when public opinion at last produced an effective Act of Parliament to curb the sale of the spirit.

The distilling of 'geneva' spirit (its name derived not from the Swiss city but from the juniper flavouring) was new to England. It was the consequence of the French wars, which prevented alike the importation of brandy and the export of English grain, then usually in surplus. Once it was found that the unsaleable corn could be turned into cheap liquor, a vested interest was created which it took a generation of appalling social evil to bring under control. In that period London was the centre of distilling and the main consumer. Gin was made freely throughout the city and as freely distributed. In the parish of St Giles, Holborn, 506 houses out of a total of 2,000 were selling it. The cost was trifling. One may smile today at the traditional notice outside the drinking-shops, 'Drunk for a penny, dead drunk for twopence, clean straw for nothing', but the reality, expressed in infantile mortality, child neglect, broken homes, loss of employment, loss of production, crime, promiscuity, and all the other social consequences of a demoralizing

Opposite First fruits of the Gothic revival: Sanderson Miller's house at 18 Arlington Street, nicknamed 'Pomfret Castle'.

Captain Coram's Foundling
Hospital, established in 1739,
symptom of the new
humanitarianism.

addiction, was anything but a joke. The 1751 Act, following several abortive
efforts, made gin dearer and less ubiquitously available. Within a few years
it was said with relief, 'We do not see the hundredth part of poor wretches
drunk in the streets as before.'

The party, or rather the orgy, was over. Georgian London now had a
chance to make progress. Conditions might remain bad by later standards,
but to contemporary observers the improvement was striking.

Much of the basis for that improvement had been laid in the first half of
the century. Captain Coram had started his Foundling Hospital in 1739,
Henry Fielding had taken his seat as Bow Street magistrate in 1749 and begun
his fight against crime, and several of the most famous general hospitals were
established in this period, the Westminster in 1719, Guy's in 1723, St
George's in 1734, the London in 1740, and the Middlesex in 1745. For the
first time there was organized help for women in childbed and a separate
Lying-in Hospital opened in 1749. Its statistics reflect the steady improvement in other fields: in the next half-century maternal mortality fell from 1 in
42 to 1 in 913, while for infants the rate changed from 1 in 15 to 1 in 115. Such
progress would never have been possible if the gin-drinking had not been
curbed.

The appearance of the streets, on which so many foreigners commented
favourably, was due to the powers now gradually acquired by the parishes,
or 'vestries', which, until local government on modern lines was introduced,
enabled the population, now something like a million, to take and feel some
responsibility for their own neighbourhood. It was the vestries, following the
lead of Westminster, which undertook the policing, lighting, paving and
cleansing of their own streets. Those streets now had their names clearly dis-

played and each house was numbered. As the pressure of traffic increased, the city gates – unnecessarily rebuilt after the Great Fire and now constituting notorious bottlenecks – were at last removed.

Gradually perhaps to our eyes – even imperceptibly, unless we study such devoted modern researches as Dorothy George's *London Life in the Eighteenth Century* – but far more noticeably to the men who lived through those decades, George III's capital changed into a more orderly, less brutal and less sordid city than his grandfather had known.

Plans for a Most Polished Gentleman

'Either the most polished gentleman or the most accomplished blackguard in Europe – possibly both.'

Such was the forecast for the future Prince Regent, made when he was only fifteen by his tutor, Bishop Hurd. Contemporary Londoners inclined rather to the second view, perhaps unjustly and certainly ungratefully. For, unpopular as the boy grew up to be, hissed in the streets and stoned when he drove to open Parliament in 1817, the city owes much to him.

In strict constitutional terms the Regency was a very brief interlude. Though mooted as far back as 1788, when George III had his first, passing attack of 'insanity' – now thought to have been porphyria, a dreadful and incapacitating condition tragically unknown to the well-meaning doctors of the time – his son did not actually become Prince Regent until February 1811, when it was evident that the King would never be fit to rule again. He died in January 1820, and the Prince succeeded as George IV, so that the Regency had lasted just under nine years. But insofar as the Prince had already dominated London society for a whole generation, and continued to do so for another decade, the same man merely confirmed in his position by a crown, it is convenient to use the word 'Regency' in an extended sense to cover the fashionable taste, style and morals between the end of the eighteenth century and the advent of Victoria in 1837.

The era began, essentially, when in 1783 the Prince of Wales, as he then was, attained his twenty-first birthday and was given his separate establishment at Carlton House, where the terrace of that name now stands, overlooking the Mall. Here, continuing the Hanoverian pattern of father-and-son animosity, he created a rallying point for the opposition, the more provocative because he differed not only in politics but in almost every conceivable way from 'Farmer' George, the King being sober, unintellectual, and a pattern of domestic virtue, while the Prince was flamboyant and wildly extravagant, an enthusiastic if erratic patron of culture, and the target for even more scandalous gossip than he deserved. In his teens he had set up Mary Robinson as his mistress, a beautiful young actress but older than himself, and married. His subsequent attachment to Mrs Fitzherbert, also older and twice a widow, was quite different. Had she not been a Roman Catholic, their secret marriage in 1785 could have been valid in English law as well as religion. It was the nearest thing to a stable personal relationship that the Prince was to enjoy, but after ten years he had to enter into a public, dynastic union, the ill-fated marriage with Princess Caroline of Brunswick which virtually ended with the birth of their only child, Charlotte. So, for almost

Opposite Polished gentleman or accomplished blackguard? The Prince Regent, later King George IV: portrait by Lawrence.

all that long period during which Carlton House was the apex of London society, it was a bachelor establishment.

When the Prince first took over the house, he employed Henry Holland to alter and enlarge it. Holland, a favourite architect with the Whig aristocracy, had begun as a speculative builder and done himself no harm by marrying a daughter of 'Capability' Brown. The snobbery of the age meant that almost all constructive achievement was left to men of humble origins, since gentlemen could not apply themselves to a profession. But at least that snobbery did not prevent the recognition of merit, and in England, Voltaire commented enviously, talents were 'the passport to glory'. Brown had begun as a gardener. John Soane, then busy on the long rebuilding of the Bank of England, and eventually to be knighted, was a bricklayer's son. And John Nash, born in Lambeth, had started his working life in a City office, tried his hand as a speculative builder on his own account, gone bankrupt, and accomplished nothing by the age of fifty-five, when in 1798 he won the notice of the Prince and was engaged to transform the interior of Carlton House. It is said that the Prince's initial approval of Nash was increased by the latter's marriage that year to Mary Anne Bradley, a lady whom His Royal Highness was anxious to see settled in life. Whatever the truth of that, it is unquestionable that the Prince became not only Nash's patron but his friend, and from his association with that snub-nosed, dwarfish genius incalculable benefits resulted for London.

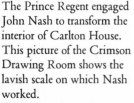

The Prince Regent engaged John Nash to transform the interior of Carlton House. This picture of the Crimson Drawing Room shows the lavish scale on which Nash worked.

In 1798 they lay far in the future. The Prince, always a spendthrift, had neither the personal means nor the political authority to provide Nash with the scope he needed. For Nash dreamed on a large scale. He was less a master of detail than, as he has been well called, 'an architectural impresario, a creator of townscape'. In those years Britain was locked in a desperate struggle

with France. It was an era of bread riots and bank failures – something like a hundred private banks failed in the single year 1810 – with a soaring National Debt and the introduction, promised as 'temporary', of income tax.

Soane, a better architect than Nash, went forward with the enlargement of the Bank, but in the City elsewhere there was no great new building in that period. Constructive effort went into other forms. It was the golden age of British sea-power, confirmed at Trafalgar. Both before and after that victory, London pressed forward with the construction of more and more docks to free the congested river and make space for the ever-expanding seaborne trade. The West India Dock in 1802, the London Dock at Wapping in 1805, the East India a year later, the Surrey Docks in 1807, followed in swift succession. Both the London and the East India were the work of a massively built Scot, John Rennie, a Lowland farmer's son, one of the new race of civil engineers. In 1811 he started what, when finished, was to be called Waterloo Bridge. Two years later he was building Southwark Bridge. And soon after his death in 1821 his sons were to carry out his design for a new London Bridge to replace Peter Colechurch's medieval structure, and, when itself superannuated in our own day, destined for transfer and re-erection in the unlikely setting of Arizona.

Docks and bridges the City could understand. Its working efficiency depended upon them, just as its trade depended on the protection of Nelson and the other admirals. On them it lavished banquets, swords of honour, gifts of gold plate. It was at the Lord Mayor's Guildhall banquet, just after Trafalgar, that the aldermen cheered Pitt's famous words: 'England has saved herself by her exertions, and will, I trust, save Europe by her example.' Such men had less use for the Prince and his fast-living set, and he had none for them. If there was one point on which he agreed with his father it was resentment against the outspoken independence of the City businessmen, still up to that date to be regarded as a progressive political force. George III, in his

The London Dock at Wapping, completed in 1805. Twenty acres in extent, it was 'conceived on a scale calculated to support the dignity of the Nation, and the important interests of its Commerce'.

The Marylebone Road, 1793, showing the open farmlands soon to be transformed into Regent's Park.

saner days, had clashed with Beckford and Wilkes. When the Prince became Regent in 1811 he carried on the feud and coldly declined the Freedom of the City.

His eyes were turned elsewhere. By happy coincidence that very year in which he achieved power saw the expiration of the Crown leases of the farmlands covering 'Marylebone Park' as it was then termed. Here was a chance for his friend Nash and for a creative partnership between prince and architect undreamt of since the days of James I and Inigo Jones.

Credit for the original conception belongs to neither. It was a Scottish civil servant with a shrewd grasp of land values, one John Fordyce, who had seen the possibilities ahead and had made sure that, when the area became free for development, there should be no obstacle. Once a part of the vanished Middlesex Forest, it was at this date split up into a typically English patch-work of fields with evocative names such as Long Forty Acre and Sparrow-hawk Wood, Rugg Moor and Further Paddock. Londoners strolled out to take the air there. The Jew's Harp was a favourite rendezvous, with its skittle alleys, its crescent-shaped tea-garden sweet with roses, its willow-fringed pool, and its upstairs room where, as dusk fell, the fiddles would strike up for dancing.

This rustic scene had little chance of surviving against the ever-growing city, 'the great wen' as Cobbett was to dub it in 1821, and the question was how, if at all, the inevitable development should be controlled, and how some of the rural charm could be kept. Fordyce had a survey made and a prize offered for the best scheme, but at that time there was little interest. Only three entries were submitted, all from one competitor, and it was not Nash, but a local resident named White, some of whose ideas Nash eventually appro-priated without acknowledgment, White being safely dead by then. In 1809 Fordyce emphasized in an official report that the value of the land in Marylebone Park would be much increased 'if means could be found to lessen the time of going from Marybone to the Houses of Parliament', and in those

The Jew's Harp tea-garden, a favoured rendezvous with its tree-shaded pool and arbours, before Nash decided that the area was ripe for development.

words he unknowingly foreshadowed Regent Street and Portland Place. A few months later he died – he was seventy-six – leaving the field wide open for Nash.

Nothing that has been said should be taken to diminish Nash's achievement. Fordyce had thought in terms of land values. Other values were Nash's prime concern. The park must, he declared, 'contribute to the healthfulness, beauty and advantage of that quarter of the Metropolis', providing 'the attraction of open Space, free air and the scenery of Nature, with the means and invitation of exercise on horseback, on foot and in Carriages . . . as allurements or motives for the wealthy . . . to establish themselves there.' For these desirable residents there would be elegant villas so disposed that each should be invisible from its neighbours, and every householder should enjoy the illusion that the panorama outside his window belonged to him alone. That panorama would be improved by the excavation of a lake, the building up of artificial hillocks, and the planting of noble trees. Social cachet would be finally guaranteed by a villa built for the Regent himself, whose title would be given to the whole park. Round its perimeter there would be terraces dressed up to look, from a distance, like single palaces. Behind them, on the eastern side, there would be humbler housing and shopping facilities, with markets supplied by a canal running from the Grand Union at Paddington to the Thames at Limehouse. Such a canal had been discussed ten years earlier, and Rennie had been interested, but it was left to Nash, with his flair for picking up other men's neglected ideas, to incorporate it into his grand design. Eleven million bricks were made from the earth dug out of the canal basin, and some of them most appropriately went to build a house for Nash himself – not in Regent's Park but in Regent Street, the great new north-to-south thoroughfare adapted from Fordyce's original suggestion. Now it was a processional way pointed not at Parliament but at Carlton House.

Not all of Nash's plans were realized. The Regent's own villa was never built, and his scheme for Trafalgar Square, as an extension of the processional

Above The Quadrant, and part of Regent Street, 1828.

Right Nash's plan for Regent's Park (shown in black). To the south a processional way was planned, to lead, by way of Portland Place and Regent Street, to Carlton House.

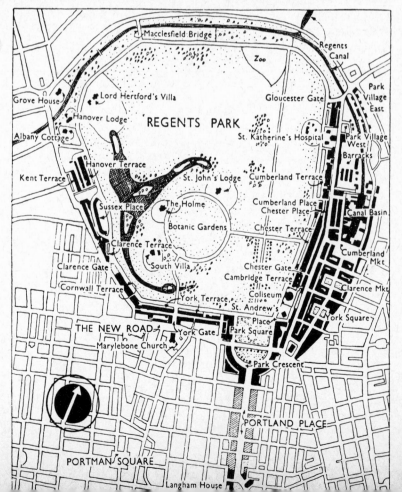

way, was carried out only after his death. Many of the Regent's Park houses were designed by Decimus Burton and other architects. But Nash did more than enough to earn our gratitude. His was the inspired conception, and despite the support of his royal patron, who promised in 1811 to outdo in London what Napoleon had done in Paris, he had to fight for it against the fiercest opposition, in and out of Parliament and sometimes at great financial risk. He was that rare phenomenon, a planner who staked his own money. His early experiences as a speculative builder may have helped: recollections of his own bankruptcy long ago can hardly have done so. In 1818, when the park was in a chaos of transformation, Henry Crabb Robinson wrote in his diary: 'This enclosure, with the new street leading to it from Carlton House, will give a sort of glory to the Regent's government, which will be more felt by remote posterity than the victories of Trafalgar and Waterloo. . . .' It was a reasonable prophecy.

When the Regent became King, he was at first content to remain at Carlton House. But he was a capricious man and before the finishing touches could be put to his processional approach he announced that a monarch could not live in a street and that the house, on which he had lavished so much, was no better than a slum. Nash was by this time seventy-three and some might have felt that he deserved a rest. Not so. Buckingham House, which George III had bought at his accession but seldom used, must now be turned into a palace fit for a king. The conversion proved expensive and was suspended in 1829, the year before George IV died, when Nash was at last allowed to enjoy a few years of retirement until his own death in 1835. Most of his work at Buckingham Palace is obscured by later additions,

Buckingham House, built in 1703, remodelled later as Buckingham Palace by Nash for George IV.

though garden-party guests can view the west façade. More accessible is his imposing entrance gate, which proved too narrow for the state coach and was relegated to the end of Oxford Street. There, as Marble Arch, it provides a useful landmark and a reminder that even the greatest of us can make silly mistakes.

There is an equally interesting survival in the pillars fronting the National Gallery, an art collection which we owe largely to George IV's vigorous initiative. When it moved to its present home, eight years after his death, William Wilkins incorporated the columns saved from Carlton House when Nash had to demolish it and replace it with Carlton House Terrace.

Nash was certainly given no respite in those final years. His master wanted not only Buckingham Palace but St James's Park remade. The French formality of Charles II's time had degenerated into what a visiting German prince called 'a sort of meadow for cows'. Nash had to landscape it into picturesqueness and turn the straight canal down the centre into the present irregular lake. Meanwhile the King's brother, soon to become William IV, complained of 'the wretched state and dirt' of the old Clarence House. Nash had to rebuild it. Besides that, in some improbable spare moments, he designed the Haymarket Theatre and the great house in Pall Mall occupied by the United Service Club, just founded by the officers who had survived Waterloo. And all through this time, of course, the Regent's Park developments were continuing, but not without constant exertion.

Westminster Abbey, St Margaret's and the New Square, 1822.

North Country Mails at the Peacock: painting by James Pollard.

Regency London is much more than Nash, however – much more, come to that, than the Regent. Nash merely provided, especially in the later years, the superb backdrop against which a cast of immortal characters moved and talked and suffered. The theatrical analogy is apt, for was there ever a more theatrical architect than Nash, with his eye for showy effect, his concentration on surfaces rather than solidity?

There was Byron, briefly the darling of society, calling on Caro Lamb at Melbourne House in Whitehall, gracing with his sardonic presence the parties of Lady Holland and Lady Oxford and Lady Jersey, or perhaps more congenially sparring with Gentleman Jackson at his Bond Street gymnasium or chatting with Walter Scott and John Murray at the publisher's office round the corner in Albemarle Street.

Keats was a medical student, dissecting at Guy's and St Thomas's. Lamb was at his desk in the India Office. Shelley was debating philosophy at Godwin's house in Clerkenwell and very soon eloping with his daughter, Mary. Harriet, the hapless first Mrs Shelley, was drowning herself in the Serpentine. De Quincey was riding out of town on the night mail, sometimes carrying the first news of a victory over the French, 'horses, men, carriages, all . . . dressed in laurels and flowers, oak-leaves and ribbons'. And after 1815, if there was no more occasion for laurels, the victor himself could be seen setting forth from Apsley House for his daily ride in Hyde Park.

Lawrence was painting portraits of all the allied leaders, a commission from the Regent himself. Constable was making his name, moving from Russell Square to Charlotte Street and then to Hampstead. Turner, son of a Covent Garden barber, had made his, and from 1811 lived out his last forty years as an irascible recluse in Queen Anne Street amid the litter of nearly twenty thousand discarded sketches.

Kean was electrifying audiences at Drury Lane, though Sarah Siddons made her professional farewell at Covent Garden in 1812, retiring to a country cottage with lattice windows and honeysuckle close to where Paddington Station now stands.

London was peopled with characters who are still household names. There was Beau Brummell, whose unshakeable self-confidence and deliberately exaggerated affectation enabled him to impose himself on the highest society as the arbiter of taste. There was Crockford, the erstwhile fishmonger, who cashed in on the aristocratic taste for gambling, amassed a million pounds for himself out of their follies, and retired to Carlton House Terrace. There was Fortnum, once a footman to George III, who had gone into trade and in 1817 entered into a famous partnership with a grocer named Mason. Swan and Edgar joined forces in Regent Street as soon as it was built. Debenham, the draper, and Gunther, the Berkeley Square pastrycook, were already in business. Two Regency firms still occupy their old St James's Street premises, Lock's the hatters and Berry's the wine merchants, though the latter were then grocers, famous for tea, coffee and snuff. Hatchard's were selling books from the beginning of the century and by 1819 the Burlington Arcade offered the quality its sheltered facilities for 'the leisurely and agreeable spending of money'. Thomas Lord had started the Marylebone Cricket Club as long ago as 1787: when Nash's canal project displaced him, he removed – turf and all – to the present 'Lord's' in St John's Wood. Another of our familiar names is Madame Tussaud: a refugee from the French Revolution in 1802, she opened her first waxworks exhibition in the Strand.

Beau Brummell, self-appointed arbiter of taste.

There is no need to lengthen the list. Regency London extended far beyond the world of Brooks's and White's and Boodle's, the clubs that had evolved from the less exclusive coffee-house society of the previous century – far beyond Almack's Assembly Rooms in King Street, where the most respectable ladies might be seen, or the rival parties of the Wilson sisters, Harriet and Amy, where they certainly might not. Outside such overlapping circles, fashionable or notorious or both, but numerically limited, there were a million other Londoners going about their business in their own way.

Princess Lieven, introducing the waltz at the Russian Embassy, was not the only innovator, though perhaps the most attractive. Other changes were crowding in, prosaic but important to the life of the city. Trevithick was demonstrating his locomotive behind a circular palisade at Euston Square, and a German enthusiast, Friedrich Albrecht Winzer, was bringing gas-light to the streets. The year of Waterloo saw the first steamers on the Thames. Towards the end of George IV's reign, in 1828, Lord Brougham and a group of other benefactors opened the college in Gower Street which was the precursor of London University, and in that same year the Zoological Gardens were added to the amenities of Regent's Park. The first omnibus

was running from the Bank in 1829, but the King did not live to see the introduction of a vehicle which would have appealed more to his taste, the intimate little cab invented by Mr Hansom in 1834.

It was a not unfitting symbol for the discreet Victorian era that was now at hand.

The Egyptian Hall, Piccadilly. Here, in 1797, John Hatchard opened the bookshop which still sells books on the same site.

Heart of Empire

It was at Kensington Palace that the eighteen-year-old Victoria was roused from sleep one June morning in 1837 to be told that she was now Queen of England. A month later the untried girl, who had been astonishing everyone with her quiet decisiveness since that first moment, ordered the removal of her establishment to Buckingham Palace, which has been the sovereign's official residence ever since.

The accommodation was far from ideal. George IV's schemes remained unfinished, and, though a certain amount of work had been done in the meantime, the building was still appallingly uncomfortable and inconvenient. Victoria, however, declared herself much pleased with her rooms. She was fond of 'the poor old palace' at Kensington where she had been born and brought up, but she was even more anxious to emphasize the end of her mother's domination. Apart from other advantages the move provided an excuse to install the indignant Duchess of Kent in a quite separate suite of apartments. For the rest, the problem of turning Buckingham Palace into a habitable and sensibly run establishment was deferred until Prince Albert came upon the scene to tackle it.

The drawbacks of the royal home, though by no means negligible, were minor compared with those of most other Londoners.

The 'great wen' continued to spread. The population had roughly doubled since 1800. Between that date and Victoria's death in 1901, it was multiplied by five. In the confines of the original City it had already begun to fall: the rich no longer cared to live there and the workers could not afford to occupy sites more profitably used for warehouses and offices. Yet until the coming of the suburban railways there was a limit to the distance they could travel to work, especially when hours were so long. An office day might run from nine in the morning until nine or ten at night. Some shops were open from eight a.m. until eleven p.m., and it was not until 1886 that any legal limit was imposed on the hours worked by the younger assistants. Only the under-eighteens were protected – any interference with the conditions of adults would have been an infringement of individual liberty unthinkable to a robust Victorian – and even the adolescent had no legal complaint until he had exceeded seventy-four hours in the week. These were the accepted conditions in reputable establishments. The hours worked in the sweat shops are unimaginable. So – although there were also conscientious and indefatigable individuals who tramped extraordinary distances daily to their work – the combination of long hours and low wages compelled far too many people to

Opposite The dark side of Victorian London: engraving by Gustave Doré, *c.* 1870.

crowd into 'rookeries' as cheap and as close to their employment as they could find.

'May we beg and beseech your proteckshion and power,' pleaded fifty-four of these unfortunates in a joint letter addressed to *The Times* in 1849.

We are Sur, as it may be, livin in a Wilderniss, so far as the rest of London knows anything of us, or as the rich and great people care about. We live in muck and filthe. We aint got no privez, no dust bins, no drains, no water splies. . . . We al of us suffer, and numbers are ill, and if the Colera comes Lord help us. . . .

The cholera came. That year it killed over fourteen thousand people in London. Five years later it returned, and another ten thousand died. These epidemics merely dramatized a continuous misery that was otherwise largely ignored. Thus, in 1842, a survey of the parish of St George's, Hanover Square, revealed that 1,465 families were sharing 2,174 rooms. These conditions could have been matched in many parts of the city. Countless people indeed had no certain shelter at all, and slept rough in any corner they could find. It was the children in this plight who impelled a young Irish doctor in 1866 to found Barnardo's Homes. About the same time William Booth was starting the movement that became the Salvation Army and did so much to expose the truth about 'darkest London'. Even earlier than Barnardo or Booth, Lord Shaftesbury had begun his long career of reform, commemorated in Piccadilly Circus by the winged archer inaccurately known as 'Eros', who is in fact intended to represent the more respectable 'Angel of Christian Charity'.

It was not strictly true, as the despairing slum-dwellers complained to *The Times* in 1849, that nobody knew or cared about their situation. There was Edwin Chadwick, irascible, tactless, pertinacious, a benevolent busy-body if ever there was one. As a young barrister, without private means, he had had the good fortune to become Jeremy Bentham's personal assistant when that great man was in his eighties. Bentham soon died, but not before he had assessed Chadwick's qualities and earmarked a handsome legacy, which endowed the young man for a lifetime of independent research and agitation. That was in 1832. By 1848 Chadwick had pushed the Public Health Act through Parliament, after years of struggle against inertia, ignorance and vested interests. He was a man who liked his own way, was mortally offended when his views were not adopted, and had no conception of making friends and influencing people. He advanced heretical opinions – he thought that public officials should be recruited by examination and decisions made by trained experts rather than elected representatives. It is not surprising that his knighthood was conferred only shortly before his death at ninety. The wonder is that he achieved so much against opponents who found his attitude even more offensive than the social evils crying out for cure.

Very different, but hardly less influential in his own way and certainly more congenial to many, was Henry Mayhew, the joint founder and editor of *Punch*, who like A. P. Herbert in the next century did not allow a sense of humour to blunt his indignation against injustice. It was in 1851, the year that fashionable society flocked with the rest of the population to admire the achievements of trade and industry in the Great Exhibition in Hyde Park,

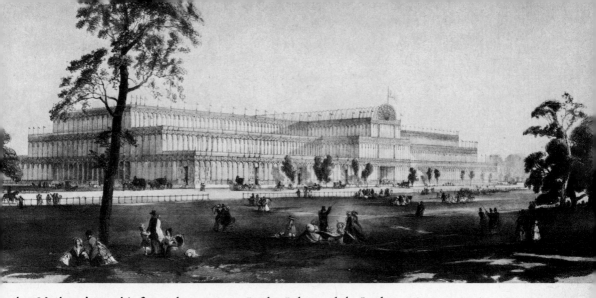

that Mayhew began his four-volume survey, *London Labour and the London Poor*, revealing the other side of the medal. It was not a bright one. Mayhew gave the ugly, unanswerable facts to reinforce what Dickens had already sketched in fiction.

So far as housing conditions were concerned it was the growth of population, not public indifference, that was most to blame. The Victorian era in London was one of dynamic constructive effort. The amount of house-building was impressive, and it was, though speculative and profitable, by no means all poor in quality by the standards of the time. The most famous of the developers was Thomas Cubitt, a carpenter's son who earned the nick-name of 'the Emperor of the Building Trade' and at his death in 1855 left, in the lengthiest will on record, more than a million pounds. Cubitt came to the fore as the Napoleonic wars were ending, and profited by the expansion that came with peace. While Nash was busy with Regent's Park, Cubitt was occupied elsewhere. Nash was the visionary, Cubitt the practical man. Cubitt's great innovation was to break away from the traditional small-scale business methods of the trade and achieve independence of sub-contractors: he was the first to create one vast, many-sided organization, employing his own tradesmen in every branch and maintaining his own fleet of horse-and-wagon transport. He acquired brickyards. He collected a team of civil engineers and was able to undertake not only housing schemes but roadmaking and drainage. Though he had no park to inspire him, as Nash had, he was at least the creator of Belgravia and a good deal of Bloomsbury, and even where he was not himself engaged in building he was much consulted by public bodies needing advice on town-planning and construction methods.

'I am much grieved by the death of that excellent and worthy man, Mr Thomas Cubitt,' the Queen wrote in her diary. 'In his sphere of life, with the immense business he had in hand, he is a real national loss. A better, kinder-hearted or more simple, unassuming man never breathed.' She had personal knowledge of his work, for he had carried out extensions to Buckingham Palace.

The Crystal Palace in its first home, Hyde Park, where it housed the Great Exhibition of 1851.

Prince Albert, of course, had been deeply concerned with better housing for the working class, and his model dwellings had attracted much notice at the Great Exhibition. The idea of flats came in about the same time, and, though conceived originally for the benefit of the poor, quickly became fashionable with wealthier Londoners. A few years later, in 1864, Octavia Hill began her career in housing reform. She started modestly, buying three cottages in Marylebone with Ruskin's help and encouragement. Then the Countess of Ducie entrusted her with the management of a property in Drury Lane, and her work snowballed until she was the benevolent controller of six thousand rented dwellings and tenements in different parts of London.

All these efforts could not keep pace with the rise in population, and sometimes the very improvements created worse problems.

This was particularly true of sewage. Chadwick was a champion of the water-closet, which had undergone various modifications in the late eighteenth century and, now that the better sort of London house had piped water, could be installed generally. Chadwick crusaded to get rid of the old cesspools and replace them with main drainage. The work began in 1849, the cholera year. Unfortunately, the sewers were taken straight down to the convenient river, and soon the Thames was polluted as never before. An unusually hot dry June in 1858 produced 'the Great Stink' when people had to hurry across Westminster Bridge with handkerchief clapped over nose and mouth, and the hirers of pleasure craft, instead of making a fortune in such weather, laid up their boats for lack of custom. The Commons had to conduct their debates behind curtains soaked in chloride of lime, while the Law Courts, not yet removed to the Strand, were almost driven out of London altogether.

At least the authorities had not been entirely taken by surprise. In the previous year they had enlisted Thomas Hawksley, the great water engineer, to help their own chief engineer, Joseph William Bazalgette, and the trio was completed by George Parker Bidder, a Devonshire stonemason's son whose genius for calculation had made him a child prodigy and whose versatility extended to every branch of civil engineering. Their solution of the problem was bold and imaginative: a main sewer should be built alongside

This cartoon by George Cruikshank shows how Prince Albert's great conception caught the public imagination.

Above Working-class
tenements in Petticoat Square
– forerunners of today's high-
rise buildings. They were
built in the 1880s.

Left Laying sewers in
Tottenham Court Road,
1845.

the river to intercept the others before they discharged their contents. Only
rainwater, in separate drains, would go direct into the Thames. The sewage
would be taken right down to the estuary before it was released.

Such a sewer would have been impracticable but for another scheme with
which it could be neatly combined. This was the construction of a new road
and embankment along the untidy and neglected waterfront. Wren had
suggested it long ago, but it was left to Bazalgette to carry it out. Between
1864 and 1870 he constructed the mile-and-a-half riverside highway, with
the sewer under it, from Westminster Bridge, just rebuilt in 1862, to Blackfriars Bridge, itself replaced in 1869. At this point the road curved away to
cut a ruthless swathe, more than half a mile long, through the old city. This
new thoroughfare, Queen Victoria Street, led to the Mansion House and
thus completed a continuous processional route from Westminster. At the

The coming of steam inspired fanciful ideas for its adaptation to carriages and even tricycles.

same time the mile-long Albert Embankment with its charming dolphin lamp-posts was completed up-river on the Surrey side. The Houses of Parliament, rebuilt by Sir Charles Barry in late Gothic style after a catastrophic fire in 1834, had been part of the panorama for the past twenty or thirty years.

Such fires were still a feature of London life and contributed to the rapid change of scene. There had been one at the Royal Exchange in the second year of Victoria's reign. In 1861 there was a great blaze in the Tooley Street warehouses on the south bank, when the Thames itself flared with a film of burning tallow. That disaster, the worst since 1666, led to the formation of a public fire service, previously left to the insurance companies. Even then, it might take the firemen half an hour to manhandle their appliances to a building only a mile away. Within a year of its foundation, the Metropolitan Fire Brigade was tested by a destructive fire at St Katharine Dock. There was another in Cheapside in 1882 and one at Tooley Street again in 1891 that burned for three weeks.

Yet all these disasters did far less to sweep away the old London than the forceful schemes of progress and profit, above all, the railway-builders. As Sir John Summerson pointed out in the opening words of his Walter Neurath Memorial Lecture in 1973, 'in the seventh decade of the nineteenth century, London was more excavated, more cut about, more rebuilt and more extended than at any time in its previous history.' The new embankments, bridges, thoroughfares and sewers already mentioned were only part of the achievement of that frenziedly constructive decade.

London had had railway termini from the beginning of the reign – indeed, London Bridge Station had been opened in 1836. Others had quickly followed, Paddington in 1838 and Fenchurch Street, the first in the City, in 1840. So it had gone on, with Euston in 1846 and Waterloo in 1848, and it

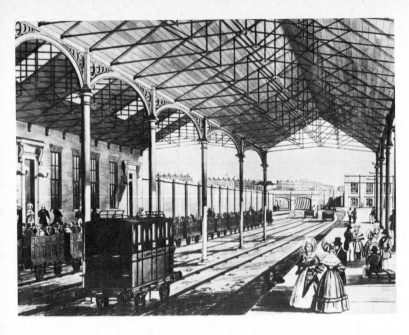

Interior of Euston Station, opened in 1846.

had been largely the cheap railway excursions that had turned the Great Exhibition into a national rather than a London affair. King's Cross had been opened the following year, 1852, by which time both Paddington and London Bridge were already undergoing reconstruction. But it was in the 1860s especially that the railway companies made their most spectacular invasion of the city, building their own bridges across the Thames and carving their way destructively into the very heart of the capital. Victoria Station became, in 1860, near neighbour to the palace of the Queen. Four years later came Charing Cross Station and Blackfriars, then Broad Street in the City in 1865 and Cannon Street in 1866. At the foot of Ludgate Hill, in the shadow almost of St Paul's, the London, Chatham and Dover Railway Company built a decorative bridge to carry its trains high above the traffic to a new terminus at Holborn Viaduct. The Viaduct itself was of course for road traffic, 1,400 feet long and a majestic 80 feet wide, bridging the valley of the Fleet. It was built between 1867 and 1869, and involved the demolition of four thousand dwellings.

These herculean achievements – all carried out, we must remember, by armies of navvies with only the simple equipment of the period – by no means complete the list. January 1863 saw the opening of the world's first underground railway, with steam trains serving seven stations on a four-mile line linking Farringdon Street with Paddington. Above ground, the decade closed with the building of yet another main-line terminus, Gilbert Scott's fantastic St Pancras, begun in 1868. All these stations, sidings, tunnels, viaducts and cuttings meant the destruction of countless homes and small businesses. The displaced multitudes were mostly tenants, with no legal claim to compensation, though they sometimes received small voluntary payments, and with no certainty of alternative accommodation, though in theory the railway companies were supposed to provide it.

In a general sense they did, by making it possible for the wage-earner to live further from his place of work. To the horse-drawn omnibuses and trams was now added a network of suburban railway lines, creating dormitory areas. In 1893 Zola, a flamboyant and most unsuburban-looking figure in his white billycock hat and flashing jewellery, was appalled by the train journey he made to Wimbledon, with 'the mean, dusty streets, lined with little houses of uniform pattern' and 'the frequently recurring glimpses of squalor and shabby gentility'. Why were the houses so small, he demanded, why were they all so ugly and so much alike?

Zola himself was staying at the Savoy, which was more to his taste. In the morning, he recalled, 'when I went to the window of my room I noticed the mist parting – one mass of vapour ascending skyward, while the other still hovered over the river, and, in the rent between, I espied a lion, poised in mid-air. It amused me vastly; and I called my wife, saying to her, "Come and see, here's the British Lion waiting to bid us good-day."' It was no mirage, but the emblem of the Lion Brewery, a famous landmark until 1948, when it was swept away to make room for the Royal Festival Hall.

Hotels such as the Savoy were another direct consequence of the railway age. In earlier centuries visitors to London had slept at coaching inns or taken lodgings for a lengthy stay. Hotels had come in about the time of the Regency, usually run by some enterprising upper servant retired from 'good' service and using his savings to take over a house in the West End. One such establishment was opened in Brook Street in 1808 and soon afterwards acquired by a Mr Claridge, who quickly built up its reputation. By 1848, 'the year of revolutions' in Europe, it was rumoured that the Pope, a fugitive from the Roman Republic, might seek refuge there. Mr Claridge said it might be difficult, he had so many royalties already in residence, though possibly, he added blandly, as His Holiness was a bachelor he might not require so many rooms. Pius IX never came, but Mr Claridge never lacked for other famous guests.

His was merely an outstanding example of those early hotels, which were essentially comfortable, old-fashioned 'family' establishments, even if at the highest social level. There were Cox's in Jermyn Street, Warren's in Lower Regent Street, Garland's off the Haymarket, favoured by the country gentry and later by Henry James, Morley's in Trafalgar Square, where South Africa House now stands, and Brown's in Dover Street which happily survives. The Tavistock, occupying one of Inigo Jones's old porticoed houses in Covent Garden, was the rendezvous of ships' captains when ashore.

Such hotels did not change the face of London. The big new ones that sprang up at the railway termini did. The Great Western at Paddington, finished in 1853, liberally turreted like a French château, with Tudor trimmings and a classical interior, was really the first of the 'modern' hotels. It soon had rivals at other stations, King's Cross a year later, Victoria in 1860 and the Gothic mass of St Pancras in 1868. Railway hotels of this type inspired the building of others, unconnected with the termini, and setting still higher standards of modern convenience. The luxury hotels, however, belong mainly to the closing years of Victoria's reign. Such was the Savoy, standing on the site of John of Gaunt's palace, with D'Oyly Carte's theatre of the

The Lion Brewery,
Southwark, whose emblem,
seen from the Savoy Hotel,
so amused Zola. The lion
now stands outside County
Hall.

Semi-detached houses in
Peckham. Built in 1866 for
the new breed of commuting
wage-earners at a cost of
£2,000 the pair, they have
long since been demolished.

195

The old Grosvenor Hotel, by Victoria Station. Built in 1860, it was designed by James Knowles on the lines of an outsize French château.

same name, built in 1881, opening from its forecourt. Such was the Cecil, built in 1896, then with its thousand rooms probably the biggest hotel in the world: its glory was short-lived, demolished in sixteen weeks in 1930 to make way for Shell-Mex House. There was the Carlton, too, dating from 1899, to which the renowned César Ritz removed himself in high dudgeon after quarrelling with the Savoy. The Ritz Hotel itself belongs to the next century – it rose on its Portland stone arcade in Piccadilly in 1904 and was one of the first steel-framed buildings in London. By then Ritz's own star had set. He never fully recovered from the nervous breakdown caused, it is said, by the postponement of Edward VII's coronation, when the new monarch was stricken down by a hitherto little-known complaint, which promptly became fashionable as 'appendicitis'.

Ostentation was by this time perhaps the keynote of London. Nash's style had been theatrical, but it had been a genuine style. With honourable exceptions the later architectural additions were pretentious and imitative. The offices of Pear's Soap were a fair example in 1894 of the 'prestige' building favoured by banks and commercial companies ever since: its hall was designed in the manner of a Pompeian atrium. The City suffered especially from demolition and reconstruction, a process that is sometimes wrongly imagined to have started only in our own day. It has been estimated that of the buildings standing in the City in 1855 only one in five remained in 1905. Casualties included Sir Paul Pindar's house in Bishopsgate Street, built in James I's reign and pulled down by the Great Eastern Railway Company in 1890, when its carved oak frontage was happily rescued by the Victoria and Albert Museum.

The City, the central square mile that had once been synonymous with London, was changing its character in other ways. It was a place of work only. Its daytime multitudes, from high financier to humble clerk, came in from distant homes outside. When they departed, it was a ghost town, peopled only by office cats and caretakers. The civic pomp survived, the sense of community was dead. Conscious, indeed over-conscious, that their City was the heart of the greatest empire the world had ever seen, the aldermen forgot that it was also, as it had been throughout history, the heart of England's largest town. In that sense they let it petrify.

In pre-Victorian times, up to the Parliamentary Reform Act of 1832, London had been the champion of political progress and liberty, and many a Lord Mayor and alderman had suffered for his courage. Then there was a reversal of attitude. The predominant mood was one of a timid and jealous clinging to forms and privileges, a stubborn opposition to the changes adopted in the rest of the country. The Municipal Corporations Act of 1835, the foundation stone of modern local government, expressly excluded London. While provincial cities such as Birmingham and Manchester pressed forward to the twentieth century, London remained an agglomeration of units running their local business on almost medieval lines. The ancient City was in a strong position to take over the hegemony of the whole area that now sprawled for miles in every direction beyond its ancient boundaries and the adjacent 'liberties' it had always controlled. But, unwilling to share its power and afraid of losing a shred of its picturesque old privileges, the City fought every attempt to fit it into a rational pattern for a unified metropolis.

By 1888 Parliament realized that something had to be done. If the City still would not come into a modern London administration, even as the senior and most influential partner, the rest of London must go ahead alone – or more accurately with every other part of England. The Local Government Act of that year set up the county councils – and not merely for Middlesex, Essex, Kent and Surrey, but for the vast built-up area where they all ran together, which was now to be given separate status as the London County Council. Again, at its own insistence, the City remained outside, and in consequence lost some of its old powers, including its authority over Southwark and other outlying districts. The Lord Mayor remained, and remains, an impressive and influential national figure, but his influence no longer extended to the affairs of London as a whole. That kind of leadership went to the more prosaically titled Chairman of the London County Council, who had no gilded coach, whose name many Londoners did not remember, but who presided over a population larger than is governed by many a foreign prime minister.

It was not until 1912 that the LCC acquired its massive headquarters at County Hall at the eastern end of Westminster Bridge. But before that, by the London Government Act of 1899, the various parts of the city were transformed into metropolitan boroughs, with their own mayors, councillors, town halls and specific powers and responsibilities. There were twenty-eight of these, and in essence the proud old City had become no more than a twenty-ninth.

Destroyers and Developers

The nineteenth century, it has been said, ended not with Queen Victoria's death but with the outbreak of the first World War in 1914. So far as London is concerned, and especially in terms of everyday life and visual details, this is largely true. On the surface, the Edwardian age seemed to continue the Victorian. There was the same opulence, the same air of superiority and security. If the heart of the Empire had missed a beat after Majuba, it recovered after Mafeking, when the good news, bursting on London unexpectedly one May evening in 1900, produced a mass hysteria of rejoicing that would have dumbfounded Pepys himself. London moved confidently into the new century, still unchallengeably the greatest city in the world, with a population which had increased five times within the past hundred years and now stood at four and a half millions. 'London is illimitable,' an American diplomat had declared in the 1860s, and there seemed no reason to contradict him in 1901, or in 1961 for that matter, by which date the population had risen to eight millions.

Yet for all that continuing growth the importance of London, relative to the world's other cities, was already in decline when Victoria died, and the new century was fated to be one of painful adjustment. The tide was turning. In 1870 the total trade of the British Empire exceeded that of the United States, Germany, France and Italy put together. An impressive proportion of that trade passed visibly and materially through London itself – the shipping that loaded and unloaded in the docks multiplied ten-fold in the course of the century – and a vastly greater percentage, though it never came to the Thames, was controlled from the banks, offices and exchanges of the City, bringing profits which filtered down through financiers to shipping clerks and typewriting ladies, thereby helping to provide a livelihood for the biggest concentration of town-dwellers ever known. Long before Edward VII mounted the throne, however, the competition of other industrial nations was in full swing, and the unique domination of Britain and London was over. But the truth lay buried in dull statistics, and the Edwardian man in the street still assumed that he lived in the greatest city in the world, which would ever remain so.

This confidence was nowhere better symbolized than in the imposing new thoroughfare of Kingsway, driven boldly through an area of mean streets between Drury Lane and Lincoln's Inn Fields, and opened by the monarch himself in 1905. Beneath it ran a tunnel, which, until 1952, brought the trams jangling up from the Embankment to emerge again into the light of day in Southampton Row. Kingsway, like the curving Aldwych laid out at the

Opposite Edwardian London: hansom cabs and horse buses in the Strand.

Piccadilly Circus as it used to be, with Shaftesbury Avenue to the left and Coventry Street stretching ahead.

same time and named after the Danes inhabiting the slope a thousand years before, was too dignified for trams. It was some years before it filled up with suitably pompous buildings – the London Opera House, later the Stoll Theatre, in 1911, Australia House begun in 1911, Bush House, American-designed and named after an American businessman, Irving Bush – a huge office-block started in 1920, its grandiose archway crowned with Malvina Hoffman's sculpture – and the adjacent India House which came even later. If not positively inspiring, at least this early twentieth-century development destroyed little of much value, unlike the oft-lamented rebuilding of Regent Street during the same period, when every vestige of Nash was obliterated from the thoroughfare he had so splendidly conceived.

Elsewhere in the West End, hardly less regrettably, new hotels, department stores, office-blocks, and flats or 'mansions' (the plural usage actually dates from 1901) had begun to destroy the old character of Piccadilly, Park Lane and Oxford Street, but with low taxation and plentiful cheap servants the great town houses of Mayfair and Belgravia held their ground until Edwardian elegance perished with the outbreak of the 1914 war. The age of uniformity and regimentation had barely begun, however shrilly the dowagers complained at Lloyd George's compulsory insurance stamps for their maids. The London scene was still more varied and – quite literally – colourful than it later became. The trams and buses, run by a number of vigorously competing concerns, brightened the streets with their rival reds, blacks, browns, yellows, blues, greens, and other hues. Even the innumerable shoe-blacks did not all sport the same scarlet that marks their rare survivor now: at King's Cross they wore brown jackets and at Marylebone white, while the gentleman who strayed into the East End would have his boots polished by an eager attendent dressed in blue. The shops similarly were individual businesses, whether they were great stores like the one started by the American, Gordon Selfridge, in 1909 or little family undertakings on the corner of a side-street. The chain was a novelty, the standardized shop-front and 'house-hold name' sufficiently rare to be welcomed as a guarantee of price and quality. The Lyons teashop was the creation of the enterprising Joseph Lyons in 1894, and within twenty years there were 200 of them, competing with the 'ABC' shops of the Aerated Bread Company. But few Londoners foresaw the day when both shopkeeping and catering would slip from the hands of the myriad small men into the control of mammoth institutions.

For all the continuing poverty – the slums, the sweated labour, the bare-foot urchins, and the other undeniable social blemishes of the period – there was a genuine gaiety, a robust vitality, that pervaded every stratum of the population. The Edwardian decade was not so different from the Naughty Nineties that had preceded it. The ageing Prince of Wales had moved from Marlborough House to Buckingham Palace, but he had not emulated Prince Hal's example with any sudden change of style. Oscar Wilde had vanished from the Café Royal, but its brilliance continued undimmed, as Orpen's 1912 painting of its famous Domino Room reminds us. The joy of life was not confined to an upper-class or intellectual minority. With something like five hundred music-halls in the city, and countless public houses, the conviviality was widely spread.

Cheap fish at the kerbside, St Giles's.

So far as striking and dramatic historical events were concerned it must have seemed as though London's separate story was dwindling into a sober chronicle of municipal improvements. There were the planned state occasions of pomp and circumstance – this was truly the age of Elgar – but would London ever again be an actor, not just a background, in the drama of national history, playing a decisive role as it had done over and over again in the conflicts of earlier centuries? For a long time it seemed improbable.

There were, of course, excitements to send the newspaper-boys clattering down the streets and bawling 'Special!' Suffragettes smashed shop windows in Oxford Street and chained themselves to the railings in Downing Street. There was the legendary Sidney Street siege, when Winston Churchill, as Home Secretary, elegant in silk hat and fur coat, called out the Scots Guards and a couple of field guns to assist 750 policemen in overcoming three armed anarchists in Stepney, a quarter much favoured by the Jewish and other immigrants then flooding in from Tsarist Russia, Poland and Romania. Yet when a fragment of really significant world history was created it passed unnoticed by the Londoners of the time – when Lenin came to live in Percy Circus, off the Pentonville Road, in 1902 and quarrelled with Trotsky the following year at the exiles' conference, at which the word 'Bolshevik' was born.

When the first World War came, London's history was essentially that of Britain at large. Inevitably the capital saw the greatest demonstrations of national feeling, for in its centre lay the obvious foci, Eros and the Trafalgar Square fountains and the Buckingham Palace balcony. For four years the West End acquired an abnormal febrile gaiety, as boyish aviators and subalterns on leave tried to forget the doom they might easily meet next week. So, too, the southern railway termini became halls of tragedy, as innumerable goodbyes were said and men passed through the barriers, never knowing if this would be the last time, to board trains to carry them back to the inferno beyond the Channel.

Otherwise, London's experience of war was the general one. There were the same social phenomena, patriotic posters, food queues, women tram-conductors and railway porters, more and more people dressed in black, more and more wounded men in garish hospital blue. The first-hand acquaintance with violent death was mercifully rare. The zeppelins came over, then the German aeroplanes. In the whole war London suffered twenty-five raids, most of the bombs falling on Bethnal Green, Poplar, Rotherhithe, Peckham, Lewisham, Sydenham, Kilburn and the City itself, where the main damage was done to the Central Telegraph Office. The civilian deaths totalled less than a thousand, a small figure by the standards of the second World War but shocking enough to the dwellers of a city that had known no enemy attack for so many centuries.

Peace came in 1918, bringing boom and slump. The food queues turned to dole queues, as in time the Victory parades were replaced with hunger marches and strike demonstrations. The Unknown Warrior was laid to rest in Westminster Abbey in 1920, in earth brought from the battlefields. On the same day the stone Cenotaph was unveiled in Whitehall. Two Empire Exhibitions at Wembley in 1924 and 1925 reaffirmed the nation's

Above Then as now, Trafalgar Square was a focal point for protest. Votes for women had to come – but not until 1918, and then only for women over thirty.

Left Women railway porters were a novel phenomenon of the First World War.

Christmas shopping at Woollands in Knightsbridge, in 1922. Wartime austerity was forgotten, at least among some classes.

faith in its destiny and brought much tourist business to London, as the Great Exhibition had done in 1851: though the Empire has gone the way of the exhibition, London retains a useful stadium for sporting encounters. There was much other building in the city. New council housing estates and private speculative schemes burgeoned in the suburbs, and, if they were not precisely 'homes fit for heroes', they were welcome enough. Commercial and public buildings continued the transformation of central London – the cliff like Broadcasting House in 1931, South Africa House overlooking Trafalgar Square in 1933, monstrous new offices for the dailies in Fleet Street about the same time, and many others apart from those already noted in Aldwych and Kingsway. Byron had unwittingly summed it all up more than a century earlier: 'wealth had done wonders, taste not much.'

For one May week in 1926 London recaptured the authentic atmosphere of historical drama – a whiff, if not of 1642, at least of the Chartist crisis of 1848. This was in the General Strike, called by the Trades Union Congress in sympathy with the locked-out miners. Armleted special constables were everywhere, amateur bus-drivers took the wheel with uniformed policemen to protect them, and sometimes their cabs additionally defended with barbed wire, undergraduates and other muscular volunteers became dockers, and the supplies they unloaded were driven in convoy out of the East End, escorted by armoured cars and Grenadiers. Hyde Park became a vast emergency encampment. In the absence of newpapers the government took over the radio and published a news-sheet, the *British Gazette*, vigorously edited by

Churchill, then Chancellor of the Exchequer. The TUC countered with the *British Worker*. But the strike was a ten days' wonder, called off without any conclusion, and the parallel with the Chartist fiasco of 1848 was not inappropriate.

It was in the second World War that London's own local history once again touched the tragic greatness of earlier days.

Even before Neville Chamberlain's Sunday morning broadcast from Downing Street, declaring war on Germany, there was the evacuation of the children. This time it was not the soldiers that tearful women watched filing through the railway barriers but their own boys and girls, labelled like the suitcases they bumped against their knees, and each slung with a white cardboard carton, which might have concealed an iced cake but in fact contained a gasmask. London nerved itself for an instant holocaust such as it had been taught to expect by H. G. Wells's film, *The Shape of Things to Come*. But nothing came – as yet.

There followed the long interlude of anticlimax, the 'phoney war'. There was the black-out, there were wartime restrictions and shortages, but after a few weeks the tension relaxed. The theatres and cinemas were allowed to re-open. And, as not a bomb had fallen, the homesick evacuees came trickling back. The most conspicuous signs of war were the sandbagged doorways of important buildings, the entrances to the air-raid shelters, the disappearance of railings for metal salvage, the masked street lamps and car lights, and – oddly beautiful – the silvery barrage balloons riding high in the sunshine, to obstruct low-level air attacks. After the invasion of Scandinavia and the Low Countries, and the fall of France, a new element was added to the London scene. Foreign uniforms and voices seemed everywhere. Before 1939 there had been a great influx of civilian refugees, Jews and other anti-Nazis from Germany and Austria. But now London became the seat of several governments in exile, and along with troops from every part of the British Empire there were Free French, Norwegians, Poles, Czechs and many other nationalities. Even the shoulder-flash of little Luxembourg might be spotted as a collector's rarity.

That summer of 1940 saw the Battle of Britain, in which Hitler tried unsuccessfully to destroy the Royal Air Force and achieve supremacy by massive attacks by night and day. London suffered in the bombing, along with many other places, but the specific assault on the capital, the real 'Blitz' as it came to be called, started on 7 September, when Hitler knew he had lost the Battle of Britain and switched his objective to the paralysing of London as the nerve-centre of Allied resistance. Every night for the next two months some two hundred German bombers flew over, dropping not only high explosives but innumerable incendiary bombs, small objects which, if dealt with immediately, might be neutralized with homely shovels, sand, and stirrup-pump and pail, but undetected could set a building on fire. 'Fire-watching' became an extra task for the weary Londoner, who had to conquer any fear of heights, learn to negotiate ladders and skylights, and clamber about on office roofs. And if it was not his – or her – turn at the place of work, there was a hurried dash home by overcrowded public transport, to 'beat the black-out', and either more fire-watching duty or an unrefreshing night in the cellar,

The Battle of Britain, September 1940. Tower Bridge silhouetted against the smoke of the blazing docks.

the air-raid shelter in the back garden, or on the platform of a tube station, which became a dormitory for hundreds with nowhere safer to sleep.

Many years later, in 1974, the famous drama critic Harold Hobson recalled: 'I was in the east, and most heavily hit, part of London during every raid but two during the entire war. I saw London burn and explode round me. But, with the exception of a couple of foreign journalists, I never heard anyone express even the smallest fear or tension.' That, admittedly, was the recollection of only one man and many who lived through those days had very different experiences. There *was* fear, there *was* tension – how could there not have been? – but on the essential point there is general agreement: the people of London displayed a stoic endurance which surprised themselves and won the admiration of the world.

That autumn the City alone recorded 415 air-raid alarms. A particularly severe raid began early one Sunday evening just after Christmas. Twenty-eight incendiaries fell on St Paul's, but by a miracle the cathedral was saved. Sixty separate fires were raging in the area. 'The dome', wrote a *Times* reporter, 'seemed to ride the sea of fire like a great ship.' Another journalist, watching from the roof of the *Daily Mail* offices, saw Ludgate Hill 'carpeted in hosepipes'. Two hundred people died that night. On the north side of the cathedral sixty-three acres became a waste of smoking ash and rubble. Another hundred acres were completely devastated in other raids that autumn. At the finish, out of the City's tight-packed 460 acres, 164 were reduced to ruin.

And this was just 1940. Though the Germans turned now to Coventry and other provincial cities they by no means forgot London – it was in May 1941 that the House of Commons was almost completely destroyed. But the severest test of the Londoners' nerve came in the later years of the war, in 1944 and 1945, when new weapons were used against them. First came the V-1, the flying bomb or 'doodlebug' as the citizens dubbed it with characteristic

The Londoners and the Blitz. *Above, left* The bombs: clearing the rubble in Fore Street. *Above* Endurance: bedded down for the night in Piccadilly tube station. *Left* Flippancy: business as usual during alterations.

flippancy. It was no joke. It travelled at 400 miles an hour, carrying 2,000 pounds of explosive. Some 8,000 of these were aimed at London, killing 6,139 people and wounding 17,239 more. Still worse was the V-2, a ballistic missile, carrying a ton of explosive at a speed of 3,000 m.p.h.

London's total air-raid casualties for the war were more than thirty thousand dead and fifty thousand injured. The cost in property was incalculable. The City alone lost about a third of its buildings, including twenty churches, part of Guildhall, and many of the livery companies' halls. So much of the beauty that Wren and his contemporaries had created in compensation for one great fire had now been obliterated in another. Elsewhere in London the destruction was hardly less severe. The bombs had fallen blindly and in-discriminately, on Buckingham Palace and slum tenement and suburban villa alike.

As in 1666 the resilient Londoners began to think of rebuilding almost before the ashes were cold, and, with the recollection of opportunities lost in that earlier period, there was a tendency to defer almost too much, if possible, to the expert and the planner. One example was the early post-war enthusiasm for higher buildings than the old regulations and techniques had allowed. Aesthetic crimes were committed against the London skyline. Worse still, positive unhappiness and social problems were created by the vogue for high-rise flats. In architectural drawings and as neat little models in exhibitions they had seemed an excellent solution for the housing shortage, more economical of land and more impressive to the eye than the bad old proliferation of council houses and bungalows. What the experts learned only by painful experience, mostly other people's experience, was the conse-quence of isolating housewives, young children, and the elderly on the six-teenth floor of a concrete and glass honeycomb, and of destroying an organic local community by redistributing its members willy-nilly to standardized new dwellings on distant sites. It is easy to be wise after the event, easy to forget the appalling urgency of the problems facing London when the bombs had ceased to fall. If the planners had made no mistakes they would not have made much at all.

It was a lively, one might almost say a perky, phoenix that rose from the ashes of the holocaust. The Festival of Britain in 1951, the centenary year of the Great Exhibition, had a similar aim in affirming the nation's optimism, but it had a lighter side less conspicuous in the Victorian effort, an emphasis on gaiety and the end of wartime austerity. One of the Festival's popular legacies to London was appropriately the Battersea Pleasure Gardens, designed by John Piper and Osbert Lancaster, and including an amusement park. Another legacy, which would have appealed more to the Prince Consort's serious taste, was the beginning of a splendid cultural centre on the South Bank, to provide concert halls of various sizes, the Hayward Gallery, the National Film Theatre, and eventually the National Theatre.

The Festival celebrations were followed all too soon by the death of George VI, but in the succession of a young Queen, with the auspicious name of Elizabeth, people found a ready excuse – however ill-based on political and economic realities – to prolong their mood of optimism and persuade them-selves that a second and equally glorious Elizabethan age was at hand. The

Pedestrians only in 'swinging' Carnaby Street.

mood did not last, but for some years the world spoke, not without reason, of 'swinging London'. The city became a byword for youth and colour and informality. An obscure back-street near Oxford Circus became internationally renowned as the shopping-centre for the exhibitionist, and 'Carnaby Street' came to be synonymous with fashionable flamboyance, while a better-known thoroughfare, the King's Road in Chelsea, took the place in the public imagination which in earlier times had belonged to Piccadilly or the Strand. The historic leadership of Paris was now successfully challenged, in the new age of mass-production and economic equality, by London designers such as Mary Quant. 'Design', indeed, was the vogue word, not only in clothes but in every material aspect of life. It had been the theme of the Festival, and it was perpetuated in the Design Centre, opened in the Haymarket.

The changing face of post-war London: the Post Office Tower for television and radio-telephony. Built in 1964, it is 619 feet high. At the widest point is a slowly revolving restaurant.

The face of London was changing, not only architecturally. In these years the mini-skirt was invented, and, until the style swept the world, the city acquired yet another famous 'sight' that at once shocked and exhilarated the foreign tourist. But London itself was becoming more 'foreign'. That most English of institutions, the teashop, was replaced by the espresso coffee-bar, while for more solid fare the Londoner turned increasingly to American hamburgers, Chinese dishes, or the Italian offerings of a spaghetti house or a *trattoria*. The traditional English 'pub' or 'local', the first objective of many an overseas visitor, held its place fairly well, but too often yielded to such innovations as piped music and self-conscious decor. The permanent population of London had in any case become more cosmopolitan. The city had had its immigrant communities ever since the Gallic shipping clerks brought their tallies and tablets to the wharfs of Londinium. Now, though Europe was liberated, many of the Europeans remained, especially those Poles, Czechs, Ukrainians and others who saw a poor future for themselves behind the Iron Curtain. To these were added, increasingly, Pakistanis, Indians and West Indians, without whose labour many public services, notably London Transport, the hospitals and the main railway stations, could scarcely have carried on. There was also a more prosperous, if less numerous, type of immigrant – the more or less permanently resident American, Australian or other returning Anglo-Saxon, who found in post-war London an intellectual or artistic stimulus lacking in his own country, and a healthier survival of certain prized values, law, order, courtesy and service. Cynical Londoners might lament the decline of these qualities, but outsiders bade them count their blessings.

Despite all these human changes, however, in the make-up of the London population and the post-war way of life, it is to the rebuilding that our attention inevitably returns.

It was much more than the massive reconstruction necessitated by the fire and the explosives. As site-values soared, 'redevelopment' became the vogue, and property speculation turned a few astute individuals into mushroom millionaires. Whole areas that had escaped the German bombs were not equally lucky with the bulldozer. Planners, public and property developers often became locked in a three-sided conflict, with the public frequently finding itself in more bitter opposition to the planners, who sincerely if misguidedly sought its interests, than to the speculators who frankly sought their own. Much of this opposition was aroused by large-scale schemes, conceived in the cause of traffic flow, which inflicted misery on the local residents. No less controversial were the proposals to destroy the former character of Covent Garden, Soho, and such remains of old Bloomsbury as had survived the growth of London University.

The planners were not always wrong. When the dust of controversy and demolition has subsided, posterity may more clearly recognize their positive achievement.

Sir Patrick Abercrombie's Report had warned them in 1943, 'Megalopolis must end in necropolis, killed by its own hypertrophy,' which encased in Greek polysyllables the blunt truth that London would die if it grew too big.

The original London – the city that had been 'London' down to Tudor times – had virtually reached the necropolis stage. Its resident community had been falling for the past century. By 1951 it was a ghost town, with willowherb and ragwort rioting over the bomb-sites. Less than five thousand people remained when the office-workers had gone home. In Cripplegate, which alone had contained fourteen thousand residents a hundred years earlier, the number had dropped to forty-eight.

Some planners might have accepted this as an irreversible tendency. The authorities, however, refused to, and embarked upon an imaginative policy of a 'Living City', designed to draw people back to the oldest inhabited site of all. The new Barbican development, for example, on a bombed area of sixty acres between Aldersgate and Moorgate, was designed to include flats, maisonettes and terraced houses for 6,500. Many of these people were in 'high-rise' accommodation, for in this quarter, where land-values were phenomenal, it was impossible in every case to avoid it. The three triangular towers were in fact the highest of their type in Europe, soaring to 410 feet. The old City *had* to be rebuilt upwards. The new Stock Exchange had twenty-four storeys. The skyline was drastically changed, but in some cases public feeling was strong enough to restrict its effects. Thus, when land was reclaimed from the river between Blackfriars and Southwark Bridge and utilized for the 'North Bank Development', no tall blocks were allowed to obscure the famous view of St Paul's.

Merely to mix homes with offices would not have resurrected a 'Living City'. So, in the Barbican complex alone, the plans allowed for an arts centre with a concert hall for the London Symphony Orchestra, a theatre for the

Architect's model of the Barbican development: a new design for living, on the oldest inhabited site of London.

Royal Shakespeare Company, a lending library, and new premises for the Guildhall School of Music and Drama. They provided also hostels for students and young workers and a site for the City of London School for Girls, removed from Carmelite Street. An earlier generation would have transferred such an institution to some outlying spot. The new planners appreciated that there could be no 'Living City' without children at its centre.

This was not all done by civic enterprise or by commercial institutions deploying vast funds. There was a place for individual vision and private venture on the smaller scale. Such an individual was the actor Sir Bernard Miles, who opened his Mermaid Theatre at Puddle Dock in 1959 and quickly established it – remote though it was from the main theatreland of the West End – as a playhouse no drama-lover could ignore.

So, by degrees, the heart of London began to beat again. The City was once more a place fit to live in, and not only for those who found it handy for the office. Even a poet laureate, Sir John Betjeman, might be discovered writing in a diminutive house in the ancient Cloth Fair, settled from choice in that same square mile once trodden by Chaucer, Jonson, Milton and so many other poets before.

And there, while not forgetting the vaster London stretching for miles in every direction, full of its own schemes and dreams, it seems appropriate to break off the inevitably unfinished story. In the new Guildhall precinct, one of the many pleasant little oases allowed for in the City's reconstruction, there is a striking piece of sculpture by Karin Jonzen. It is called 'Beyond Tomorrow', and is a reminder that after nineteen centuries the Londoners are still looking forward to an interesting future.

Beyond Tomorrow by Karin Jonzen.

Painters at work, from the 12th-century Dover Bible. Cambridge Corpus Christi College MS. 4 fol. 241v. Courtesy of the Master and Fellows of Corpus Christi College, Cambridge. Photo Courtauld Institute of Art, University of London.

35 King John at a stag-hunt, from an early 14th-century illuminated manuscript. Cotton MS. Claudius D. II. fol. 116, *British Library.*

36 Bear-baiting, from the Luttrell Psalter, *c.* 1340. Add. MS. 42130 fol. 161, *British Library.*

Wrestling scene, from Queen Mary's Psalter, *c.* 1300. Royal MS. 2 B. VII. fol. 161v, *British Library.*

37 Men in prison and in stocks, from a manuscript drawing, *c.* 1175. Trinity College MS. R. 17. 1, *Trinity College Library, Cambridge.*

39 Loading a merchant ship, from a late 15th-century illuminated manuscript. Bodleian MS. Douce 208 fol. 120v, *Bodleian Library, Oxford.*

40 A king with his parliament. Initial from a 13th-century illuminated manuscript. Cotton MS. Nero D. VI. fol. 72, *British Library.*

41 The Great Seal of Henry II (1154–89). *British Library.*

42 A parliament of Edward I, from a print published 1 November 1724 by L. Herbert, 29 Great Russell Street, Bloomsbury. *Courtesy of the Trustees of the British Museum.*

43 Seal of the City of London, 13th century. *British Library.*

44 Henry III and his masons, drawn by Matthew Paris, 13th century. Cotton MS. Nero D. I. fol. 23v, *British Library.*

Westminster Abbey after Henry III's rebuilding, from 'Historia Anglorum', 13th-century manuscript by Matthew Paris. Royal MS. 14 C. VII. fol. 138v, *British Library.*

45 The Court of Exchequer, *c.* 1460, from an illuminated manuscript. *Courtesy of the Masters of the Bench of the Inner Temple Library.*

The Court of Chancery, *c.* 1460, from an illuminated manuscript. *Courtesy of the Masters of the Bench of the Inner Temple Library.*

46 A coach with noble ladies, from the Luttrell Psalter, *c.* 1340. Add. MS. 42130 fol. 181v, *British Library.*

47 The Hall, Lincoln's Inn, built during the 15th century. Photo A. F. Kersting.

49 Edward I in armour. Illuminated initial, 13th century. Cotton MS. Nero D. IV. fol. 4, *British Library.*

50 Nun playing a musical instrument, from Queen Mary's Psalter, *c.* 1300. Royal MS. 2 B. VII. fol. 177, *British Library.*

Nun and friar in stocks, from the Smithfield Decretals, early 14th century. Royal MS. 10 E. IV. fol. 187r, *British Library.*

51 Jewish moneylender, from a 14th-century illuminated manuscript. Add. MS. 27695 fol. 7v, *British Library.*

Jews being persecuted, from a 14th-century manuscript. Cotton MS. Nero D. II. fol. 183, *British Library.*

53 Edward III in robes of the Order of the Garter. Tinted drawing by Sir William Bruges (d. 1449), first Garter King of Arms. Early 15th century. Stowe MS. 594 fol. 7v, *British Library.*

54 The Black Death at Tournai, 1349, from Gilles le Muisit's 'Annales', 1352. MS. 13076–77, fol. 24v, Bibliothèque Royale de Belgique, Brussels. Photo Giraudon.

56 John Ball meets Wat Tyler outside London, from a Flemish manuscript, the 'Chroniques de France et d'Angleterre' by Jehan Froissart, *c.* 1460–80. Royal MS. 18 E. I. fol. 165v, *British Library.*

58 Funeral pall of the Fishmongers' Company, late 15th century. *Reproduced by kind permission of the Fishmongers' Company.*

59 Sixth seal of Edward III, *c.* 1350. *British Library.*

60 Richard II. Detail from the Wilton

Diptych, oil on panel, *c.* 1380–90. *National Gallery, London.*

61 Portrait of John of Gaunt, from the 'Donation Book of Benefactors of St Alban's Abbey', *c.* 1380. Cotton MS. Nero D. VII. fol. 7, *British Library.*

63 Portrait of Chaucer, from an early 15th-century manuscript of Thomas Hoccleve's 'De Regimine Principum'. Harley MS. 4866 fol. 88, *British Library.*

64 The murder of Archbishop Sudbury, from a Flemish manuscript, the 'Chroniques de France et d'Angleterre' by Jehan Froissart, *c.* 1460–80. Royal MS. 18 E. I. fol. 172, *British Library.*

65 Wat Tyler threatening Richard II, from a Flemish manuscript, the 'Chroniques de France et d'Angleterre' by Jehan Froissart, *c.* 1460–80. Royal MS. 18 E. I. fol. 175, *British Library.*

66 The Tower of London, from a copy of 'The Poems of Charles, Duke of Orleans', probably executed in England in the Flemish style *c.* 1500. Royal MS. 16 F. 2. fol. 73, *British Library.*

68 Earliest printed view of London, from *The Chronycle of Englonde*, printed by Wynkyn de Worde, 1497. Photo courtesy of the Trustees of the London Museum.

70 Westminster Hall, showing Hugh Herland's roof, 1394–1402. Photo *Country Life*, London.

72 The death-bed of Richard Whittington. A 15th-century manuscript drawing. By kind permission of the Mercers' Company.

73 Simon Eyre, Lord Mayor of London, 1445–6. Manuscript drawing. *Guildhall Library.*

Leadenhall. Detail from a copper plate engraved with the Moorfields and Finsbury section of a map of London, *c.* 1558–9, apparently the work of Franciscus Hogenberg, from sketches by A. van den Wyngaerde. *Courtesy of the Trustees of the London Museum.*

75 Fishmongers' float with artificial leopard devised for Lord Mayor's Show. 17th-century drawing. *Reproduced by kind permission of the Fishmongers' Company.*

76 Coats of arms, Skinners' Company and Merchant Taylors. *Courtesy of the Trustees of the London Museum.*

78 Portrait of Edward IV (1461–83). Oil on panel. *Society of Antiquaries, London.*

80 Title-page of the *Recuyell of the Historyes of Troye* by Raoul Lefèvre, printed by William Caxton c. 1474. Photo Henry E. Huntingdon Library and Art Gallery.

81 The squire, by Wynkyn de Worde, from Chaucer's *Canterbury Tales*, printed by William Caxton, 1485. *British Library.*

82 Portrait of Richard III (1452–85) by an unknown artist. Panel. *National Portrait Gallery, London.*

83 Wooden roof of the Great Hall, Crosby Place, built by Sir John Crosby in 1466. Photo *Country Life*, London.

84 Effigy of Henry VII, 1509. Coloured plaster. Courtesy of the Dean and Chapter of Westminster. Photo R. P. Howgrave-Graham.

84–5 View of Richmond Palace from the waterside. Drawing by Anthony van den Wyngaerde, 1562. *Ashmolean Museum, Oxford.*

87 The Charterhouse as it was in the 16th century. Engraving from *The History and Antiquities of London* by Thomas Allen, 1828. *Guildhall Library.*

88 Georg Gisze, c. 1532. Oil painting by Hans Holbein the Younger. Staatliche Museen Preussischer Kulturbesitz: Gemäldegalerie Berlin (West).

89 Vagabonds whipped at the cart's tail. Detail from title-page of Harman's *Caveat*, 1567. *British Library.*

90 Bird's-eye view of the City of London. Engraving from *Civitas Orbis Terrarum* by Braun and Hohenburg, 1573–1618. *British Library.*

91 Cheapside, showing conduit. Drawing by Ralph Treswell, 1585. *Courtesy of the Trustees of the British Museum.*

92 Bust from the tomb of John Stow (1525–1605) in the church of St Andrew Undershaft, London. Photo Edwin Smith.

93 Laundresses at work. Detail from a copper plate engraved with the Moorfields and Finsbury section of a map of London, c. 1558–9, apparently the work of Franciscus Hogenberg, from sketches by A. van den Wyngaerde. *Courtesy of the Trustees of the London Museum.*

94 Bronze medal of Henry VIII by Hans Schwartz, c. 1516–27. *Courtesy of the Trustees of the British Museum.*

97 Portrait of Sir Thomas Gresham, c. 1568. Panel by an unknown Flemish artist. *National Portrait Gallery, London.*

98 Shoe-horn inscribed 'This is Hamlet Radesdale Setteson and Coupar of Londan, Anno Domini 1593. Sarve God. Robart Mindum mad this.' *Courtesy of the Trustees of the London Museum.*

99 Ludgate, from an 18th-century print showing the ten city gates. *Guildhall Library.*

100–1 Ships on the Thames. Detail from C. J. Visscher's 'View of London', engraved in 1616. *Courtesy of the Trustees of the British Museum.*

102 Shop interior. Detail of woodcut on the song-sheet 'A Caution for Scolds' from the *Roxburghe Ballads*, Vol. 2, late 16th – early 17th century. *British Library.*

103 Sir Thomas Gresham's Royal Exchange. Engraving by Franciscus Hogenberg, 1569. *Courtesy of the Trustees of the British Museum.*

104 Old East India House, Leadenhall Street. Engraving from Brigg's *Relics of the East India Company*. *British Library.*

106 Dancing scene. Detail of woodcut on the song-sheet 'The Mystery Discovered' from the *Roxburghe Ballads*, Vol. 2, late 16th–early 17th century. *British Library.*

107 Tavern scene. Detail of woodcut on a song-sheet from the *Roxburghe Ballads*, Vol. 2, late 16th–early 17th century. *British Library.*

108 Beaufort House, Chelsea, seat of the Duke of Beaufort. Engraving by Kip, c. 1700, from *Britannia Illustrata*. *British Library.*

109 Preacher at Paul's Cross, c. 1616. Panel by an unknown artist. *Society of Antiquaries, London.*

110 Morris dancer. Detail from title-page of *Kemps nine daies wonder* by William Kemp, 1600. *British Library.*

The jester Richard Tarlton. Late 16th-century manuscript drawing. Harley MS. 3885 fol. 19, *British Library.*

111 Foot-soldiers. Detail of woodcut on a song-sheet from the *Roxburghe Ballads*, Vol. 3, late 16th–early 17th century. *British Library.*

A game of chess. Detail from the title-page of *The Famous game of Chess play* by A. Saul, 1614. *British Library.*

112–13 Bankside, showing Globe theatre and Bear Garden. Detail from C. J. Visscher's 'View of London', engraved in 1616. *Courtesy of the Trustees of the British Museum.*

114 Probable self-portrait of Richard Burbage (c. 1568–1619). Canvas, British School. *By permission of the Governors of Dulwich College Picture Gallery.*

115 Portrait of Edward Alleyn (1566–1626), founder of Dulwich College, by an unknown artist. Canvas. *By permission of the Governors of Dulwich College Picture Gallery.*

A travelling coach. Detail of an engraving by John Dunstall from *London Prospects Portfolio*, Vol. V. *Society of Antiquaries, London.*

116 Interior of the Swan theatre. Contemporary copy of the lost drawing by Johannes de Witt, c. 1596. *Universiteitsbibliotheek, Utrecht.*

117 Portrait of Ben Jonson (?1573–1637). Canvas, after A. Blyenberch. *National Portrait Gallery, London.*

118 View of London, from Southwark. Detail from Wenceslas Hollar's 'View of London', etched in 1647. *Courtesy of the Trustees of the London Museum.*

119 Elizabeth I (1558–1603). Silver medal commemorating the Spanish Armada, 1588. *Courtesy of the Trustees of the British Museum.*

120 Execution of Guy Fawkes and other conspirators in 1606. Drawing by C.J. Visscher. *Courtesy of the Trustees of the British Museum.*

121 By the Waterhouse at Islington. Etching by Wenceslas Hollar, 1665. *Courtesy of the Trustees of the British Museum.*

122 Head of the Mercers' Company Mace, by Edward Pinfold, 1679. By kind permission of the Mercers' Company. *Photo the Worshipful Company of Goldsmiths.*

123 Title-page of *The Roaring Girl* by Thomas Dekker and Thomas Middleton, 1611. *British Library.*

124 St James's Palace and part of the City of Westminster as they appeared in 1660. Engraving by Sawyer after Hollar. *Courtesy of the Trustees of the London Museum.*

Sir Paul Pindar's house, Bishopsgate Street, built *c.* 1624. Engraving by Sawyer after T. Shepherd. *Photo National Monuments Record.*

125 Suffolk House, Charing Cross, originally called Northumberland House. Engraving after Hollar, published 1808. Pepysian Library, Cambridge. *Photo National Monuments Record.*

North view of Arundel House, the Strand, 1646. Engraving by Adam Bierling after Hollar, published 1792. *Guildhall Library.*

South view of Arundel House, the Strand, 1646. Engraving by Adam Bierling after Hollar, published 1792. *Guildhall Library.*

126 Lincoln's Inn Fields. Pen and brown-ink drawing by William Lodge (1649–89). *Courtesy of the Trustees of the British Museum.*

127 Set design for Ben Jonson's masque *Oberon*, by Inigo Jones, 1611. Devonshire Collection, Chatsworth. Reproduced by permission of the Trustees of the Chatsworth Settlement. *Photo Courtauld Institute of Art, University of London.*

129 James I with his Queen, Anne of Denmark. Print by Renold Elstrack, *c.* 1603–25. *Courtesy of the Trustees of the British Museum.*

130 Charles I (1625–49) dining in public. Oil painting by Gerrit Houckgeest. Reproduced by gracious permission of H.M. the Queen.

131 Old Somerset House. Pen and ink drawing by William Lodge (1649–89). *Courtesy of the Trustees of the British Museum.*

132 Charles I's instructions to the Attorney-General, 3 January 1641–2. Egerton MS. 2546 fol. 20. King's signature from Add. MS. 39672 fol. 34v, *British Library.*

133 'The Resolution of the women of London. . . .' Woodcut from the *Thomason Tracts*, 26 August 1642. *British Library.*

134 Mount Mill, one of the forts of the City of London. Detail from a broadsheet entitled 'The Malignants trecherous and Bloody Plot against the Parliament and City of London', 1643. *Courtesy of the Trustees of the British Museum.*

135 The trial of King Charles I, 1648. Engraving. *Courtesy of the Trustees of the British Museum.*

136 Cromwell dismissing the Rump parliament, 1653. Contemporary Dutch satirical engraving. *Courtesy of the Trustees of the British Museum.*

138 Erra Pater's Prophesy, or Frost Fair, 1683–4. Engraving attributed to Faithorne. *Courtesy of the Trustees of the British Museum.*

140 Chiswick from the river. Oil painting by Jacob Knyff, *c.* 1675. *Courtesy of the Trustees of the London Museum.*

141 King Charles II. Oil painting by Sir Peter Lely, *c.* 1670. The Governor and Committee of the Hudson's Bay Company.

143 Burlington House, Piccadilly. Engraving by Kip, *c.* 1700. *Courtesy of the Trustees of the British Museum.*

St James's Square. Engraving by Sutton Nicholls, published 1754. *Courtesy of the Trustees of the British Museum.*

144 Plague bell of wood and bronze, *c.* 1666. *Courtesy of the Trustees of the London Museum.*

Tradesman's token showing the Monument, erected in 1677. *Courtesy of the Trustees of the British Museum.*

145 The Fire of London. Oil painting attributed to Willem van de Velde, *c.* 1667–70. *Courtesy of the Trustees of the London Museum.*

An early fire engine. Trade card from a print of 1678. *Courtesy of the Trustees of the London Museum.*

The destruction around St Paul's. Detail of a view of London after the Fire engraved by Wenceslas Hollar, 1666. *Courtesy of the Trustees of the British Museum.*

146 Plan for the City after the Fire of 1666. Engraving after plan by Christopher Wren. *Courtesy of the Trustees of the British Museum.*

Portrait of Sir Christopher Wren. Painting begun by Antonio Verrio (?1639–1707), finished by Sir Godfrey Kneller (?1649–1723) and Sir James Thornhill (1676–1734), *c.* 1706–*c.* 1724. Sheldonian Theatre, Oxford. *Photo Thomas Photos.*

147 The frozen Thames near London Bridge, 1677. Oil painting by Abraham Hondius (1638–95). *Courtesy of the Trustees of the London Museum.*

148 St Paul's Cathedral from the west. *Photo National Monuments Record.*

149 Montague House in Great Russell Street. Engraving published 1754 by Sutton Nicholls from John Stow, *A Survey of the Cities of London and Westminster*, 6th edition, 1754. *Courtesy of the Trustees of the London Museum.*

150 No. 22, College Hill. Front elevation of house dating from the late 17th century. *Photo Group Three Photography Ltd.*

Index